Insider Threats

Being simple is complicated

(Être simple, c'est compliqué)

Advances in Information Systems Set

coordinated by
Camille Rosenthal-Sabroux

Volume 10

Insider Threats

Pierre-Emmanuel Arduin

WILEY

First published 2018 in Great Britain and the United States by ISTE Ltd and John Wiley & Sons, Inc.

ISTE Ltd
27-37 St George's Road
London SW19 4EU
UK

www.iste.co.uk

John Wiley & Sons, Inc.
111 River Street
Hoboken, NJ 07030
USA

www.wiley.com

© ISTE Ltd 2018
The rights of Pierre-Emmanuel Arduin to be identified as the author of this work have been asserted by him in accordance with the Copyright, Designs and Patents Act 1988.

Library of Congress Control Number: 2017963958

British Library Cataloguing-in-Publication Data
A CIP record for this book is available from the British Library
ISBN 978-1-84821-972-4

Contents

List of Figures

List of Scenarios

Preface

Information is the basis of all interactions between two beings endowed with intelligence: from chemical variations between cells to the exchange of electronic signals between machines, information has been exchanged since the beginning of time. An attentive reader will question whether cells and machines are really endowed with intelligence, but what is intelligence if not our capacity to *link* ideas with each other? The word "intelligence" is in fact made up of the Latin suffix *inter-* meaning "between" and the stem *ligare* meaning "to link". Information and intelligence thus seem to converge toward this idea of linking, for any kind of being, through exchange of information, or ideas, through intelligence.

Language follows this path and so does writing: both support the exchange of information in an information system. An information system can be seen as a group of digital and human resources organized in order to process, spread and store information [REI 02]. In Europe, the Church had a strong hold on writing but, due to increasing commercial activity during the 11th and 12th Centuries, writing became more widely established and was integrated into the management of businesses and the sharing of information as a source of knowledge. In the 15th Century, Gutenberg sped up the diffusion of information by inventing the printing press. This first breakthrough was followed, at the end of the 19th Century, by another innovation when Hollerith, with the Tabulating Machine Company, did not speed up the diffusion but rather the processing of information. In order to help with the census of the U.S. population in 1890, he proposed coding information regarding each U.S. citizen on punch cards before processing them (Figure 1). Thus, information becoming processed automatically lead to the birth of computer science. At the beginning of the 20th Century, the Tabulating Machine Company became the International Business Machines Corporation: IBM.

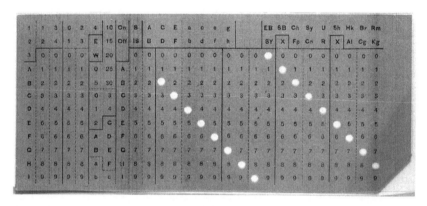

Figure 1. *A Hollerith punch card in 1890 (source: The Library of Congress, American Memory)*

The massive computerization of information systems during the second half of the 20th Century led the countries engaged in this process to reflect on the ethics and security of these systems. Indeed, Hollerith's tabulating machines would have allowed the Nazi regime to take an inventory of thousands of people and thus facilitate their deportation. In 1974 in France, the *Système Automatisé pour les Fichiers Administratifs and Répertoire des Individus* (SAFARI) project aroused strong emotions among the public when the Ministry of the Interior wanted to create a centralized database of the population with all administration and banking files. In response to this controversial initiative, the French Data Protection Authority (CNIL) was created in 1978 in order to define a framework for computer science to be "in the service of each citizen" and so that it "undermines neither human identity, nor human rights, neither private life, nor individual or public freedoms" [RÉP 78]. In the United States, the construction of models allowing designers to gain "trust" has even been tried [TCS 85]. The General Data Protection Regulation (GDPR) of 2016 is also a regulation and control initiative concerning the use of personal data.

For some people, computer science can represent a flaw in the security of information systems insofar as it processes information automatically. In addition, the security of information systems has often been looked at by focusing on artifacts, computer science and technologies. This book is meant to be timeless, just as relevant to the 19th Century as to the 21st Century; its ambition is to change this paradigm and take an interest in the security of information systems by considering individuals as components in their own right. Indeed, they are susceptible, just like a computer or any artifact, to constitute an insider threat to the information system's security.

Pierre-Emmanuel ARDUIN
January 2018

Introduction

Computing is not what it was in 1974, or even in 2006. Information systems within organizations are largely supported by underlying computer systems, whose security can be rigorously ensured through procedures, fragments of code and infrastructures.

While yesterday's punch card could be hidden during its journey between a perforator and a tabulating machine, today a piece of information, computerized, is subject to innumerable threats regarding its security. Digital artifacts are everywhere, computing is ubiquitous [NOJ 05, FRI 11], in such a way that the individual is no longer a simple user of the information system, but he or she is a fully fledged component [ARD 15]. The definition of an information system made by Reix [REI 02] integrates not only a digital component, certainly, but also a human component. The following question then arises:

How can we ensure the security of an information system while taking into account individuals as a component whose behavior may be irrational?

This book is more specifically interested in the human component of the information system, in particular because it constitutes an *insider threat* to the system's security. Security must indeed be assured not only from the point of view of digital artifacts, but also and above all from a human, social and managerial point of view. This constitutes the main originality of this book that allows the paradigm of information systems security to evolve by strongly emphasizing the insider threat, a threat that is found inside the organization itself, masters its processes, its firewall and its security policy. Whether they are intentional or accidental, malicious or not, insider threats must be identified, understood and handled, something this book proposes to do.

Between 2013 and 2015, more than 100 banks in 30 countries were the victims of cyberattacks, with losses estimated at between 300 million and 1 billion dollars, according to a report by the cybersecurity company Kaspersky Lab [KAS 15]. Most of the time, the institutions attacked kept quiet or minimized the attacks. The tools used were not extremely complex, contrary to the infiltration operation: the attackers took the time to understand the internal procedures of the targeted organization in order to target the human component. The report focuses on the malicious Carbanak software, through which the attackers proceeded to a manual reconnaissance of the victim's network in order to access its critical systems, understand its infrastructure and install remote access software. How did the attackers install Carbanak in the targeted organization? What entry point into the system did they use?

While 200 billion e-mails were sent per day throughout the world in 2015, the attackers used the *spear phishing* method. Personalized e-mails were sent to a limited number of targets judiciously chosen (see Figure I.1). Unlike *phishing, spear phishing* integrates social engineering techniques in order to win the target's trust and persuade them of the truth of the information provided. These techniques will be studied in this book and the interested reader will find them in Chapter 4.

Thus, it was actually human beings who were the entry point into the system used in the above-mentioned Carbanak attacks. Once installed, Carbanak records every keyboard tap and takes screen captures every 20 s. This information allows attackers to better know their victim and better target their next attacks.

```
Good Day!
I send you our contact details
 The amount of deposit 32 million rubles and 00 kopecks, for a period of 366
days, ? year---end contribution term
 Sincerely, Sergey Kuznetsov;
+ 7 (953) 3413178
f205f @ mail.ru
```

Figure I.1. *Example of a successful Carbanak phishing e-mail accompanied by a compressed configuration file in .rar format (source: [KAS 15])*

In an information system, the human is – just like a computer or any other digital artifact – a component of the system: he or she processes, stores and spreads information. Since the massive computerization of information systems in the second half of the 20th Century, a strong desire to secure information systems has stressed the security of underlying computer systems. This desire has, nevertheless, ignored the human component. Humans can thus constitute a threat, but focusing on the digital continues to neglect this threat, which in turn contributes to the success of the attacks. Observations that we have been able to make in the field, as well as investigations in the literature on the subject, have led us to focus on the insider threat that the human component constitutes, that is to say the employees in an organization, for the security of the information system.

This book consists of two parts. The first part presents the information system from the point of view of its components: technologies (Chapter 1), which humans have historically used for precise purposes such as supporting the exchange and processing of information in organized systems (army, commerce, then "organizations"), and individuals (Chapter 2), who are so many interpretive components whose behavior is sometimes irrational within the organized systems that they make up. These components of the information system, technologies and people, are so many entry points prone to being a threat to the security of the information system.

In addition, the second part of this book focuses all of its attention on the insider threat that the individuals who make up the information system can represent.

In Chapter 3, a classification of these insider threats is presented, then the focus will turn to each one of them individually.

In Chapter 4, unintentional insider threats are presented, where manipulation techniques and social engineering can incite an employee, a component of the system, to inadvertently facilitate infiltration by an attacker.

In Chapter 5, intentional and non-malicious insider threats are discussed, where an employee has an interest in going around the security policy of the information systems to make daily work easier but without a desire to cause harm.

Finally, in Chapter 6, intentional and malicious insider threats are presented, where the organizational context and the cognitive processes can lead an employee to want to cause harm are analyzed, as is the possibility – or lack thereof – of dissuading him or her.

A discussion of the limits and possible changes in what has been put forward in this book is finally presented in the Conclusion.

PART 1

Information Systems: Technologies and People

1

Components with
Known Purposes: Technologies

In Greek mythology, when Theseus left to fight the Minotaur, his father Aegeus asked him to replace the black sail of his boat with a white one if he returned victorious. Just like components of an information system, Theseus and Aegeus were exchanging information through a clearly defined procedure. An information system is not a computer system. Organizations can see their information system supported by a computer system, but the information system cannot be reduced to a computer system. Individuals, the users of the computer system, are components of the information system: they also process, store and spread information, whether through the computer system or not. In this way, they themselves are also entry points likely to constitute the insider threats that this book addresses.

This chapter will discuss the technologies that have been used by human beings to support and secure information systems throughout history. From the decrease in transmission time to the massification of the quantities processed, the purposes of these technologies have evolved through the years and led to the explosion of a threat that is still part of every information system: the insider threat.

It is not our intention to focus on a history of the concept of information systems, but rather on a history of artifacts and technologies implemented by human beings to support and secure it. In fact, for authors such as Weizenbaum [WEI 84]: "the remaking of the world in the image of the computer started long before there were any electronic computers". Thus, the reader will see how, over the years, these artifacts have pursued goals such as decreasing transmission time, decreasing processing time or the massification of quantities of information in an information system. Each time, these artifacts have revealed new threats to the information system's security and the history that we offer in this chapter is intended to make the reader aware of the possibility of threats that do not come from the technological component of the information system. Indeed, since the beginning of time, the human component of the information system has constituted an insider threat, as this history will demonstrate.

1.1. Up to the end of the 19th Century: decreasing transmission time

In the second Century BC, the Greek Polybius developed a system for transmitting information over long distances in a few minutes where otherwise several hours of travel on horseback would have been necessary [LAU 77]. An operator showed or hid torches behind two walls in order to represent a letter of the alphabet (Figure 1.1). In fact, Polybius proposed dividing the alphabet into five groups of letters, with the result that only two "digits" were sufficient to represent the entire alphabet. Table 1.1 shows Polybius' code: to represent an "A", a torch was raised on the first wall and another on the second (first line and first column); to represent a "Ω", five torches were raised on the first wall and four on the second (fifth line and fourth column).

Figure 1.1. *Artifacts supporting an information system in the second Century BCE ([LAU 77], source: Bibliothèque Nationale de France)*

	1	2	3	4	5
1	A	B	Γ	Δ	E
2	Z	H	Θ	I	K
3	Λ	M	N	Ξ	O
4	Π	P	Σ	T	Y
5	Φ	X	Ψ	Ω	

Table 1.1. *Polybius' code*

Independently of any artifact, an individual, from the moment he/she exchanges information, places himself/herself in an information system in which he/she is a component. In this way, the author, while writing this book, is part of an information system and the reader, when he or she reads these words, is within an information system. Information systems are everywhere and very often it has been military motivations that have motivated humanity to perfect them, thus raising the question of the security of such systems.

Indeed, talking is a natural process for human beings who are able to comprehend the risks inherent in the security of the information that spreads when they talk. For example, a child knows that he/she risks being overheard. If we can imagine what dangers might threaten a messenger on horseback in Ancient Greece, it is also possible to see security breaches in Polybius' information system: everyone has access to the information being transmitted. This awareness of security flaws is not natural for human beings insofar as the means of communication is not natural. The same thing is true when information systems within organizations are increasingly supported by digital artifacts.

From the moment it is supported by an artifact, an information system presents security flaws that we are not naturally aware of.

Although artifacts can give a false impression of security and lead to flaws that individuals must be made aware of, the fact remains that natural forms of communication can also lead to flaws that individuals must be made aware of.

Polybius perfected his system very quickly with the help of a password: one starts to fill in the square (Table 1.1) with the letters of this password and then completes it with the remaining letters of the alphabet. At the time, the message was indecipherable without the password. This kind of encryption with monoalphabetic substitution is easily decipherable today with an analysis of how frequently letters appear in a language. In French, for example, the letter "e" is the most frequently used.

There are documents attesting to the existence of systems comparable to Polybius', although simpler, used by the ancient people of Europe and Asia. For example, the Roman army established telecommunication stations along Roman roads [LAU 77]. Trajan's column in Rome provides a visual representation of these observation turrets equipped with torches (Figure 1.2). In China, the Great Wall was equipped with fires used to signal an attack. Brick cones full of wood and straw also served to create smoke to announce the arrival or retreat or enemy troops.

Figure 1.2. *Artifacts supporting the Roman army's
information system in the first Century*

In the Middle Ages, the Romans' system fell into disuse in Europe while in Constantinople, signal lights remained in use for signaling Muslim incursions. Progress in physics in the 16th and 17th Centuries rekindled the idea of systems that could transmit information over distances at "great speed". In France in 1705, the Royal Academy of Sciences wrote the following about the system of physicist and academician Guillaume Amontons:

> "[Amontons' system] consists of having several people in consecutive posts who, by means of telescopes, having seen certain signals from the previous post, transmit them to the following one, and so on, and these different signals are the letters in an alphabet whose code is known in Paris and in Rome. Most of the telescopes cover the distance between the posts, whose number must be as low as possible; and the same way the second post sends signals to the third as soon as they see the first post sending it, the news is sent from Paris to Rome in as little time as it took to send the signals in Paris". [FON 05, p. 152]

The telegraph of the Chappe brothers (Figure 1.3) followed at the end of the 18th Century and was the first telecommunications network with a national scope. By defining the conventions and vocabularies, the Chappe brothers made it possible to link very precise signals to specific dispatches especially applying to the army. Figuier [FIG 68] explains how it works:

> "The telegraph itself, or the part of the machine which creates the signals (fig. [1.3]), is made up of three mobile branches: a main branch AB, 4 meters long called the *regulator* and two small

branches 1 meter long, AC, BD, called *indicators*, or *wings*. Two iron counterweights *p*, *p'* attached to a rod of the same metal, balance the weight of the *wings*, and making it possible to move with very little effort. These rods are somewhat thin so they are not visible from a distance. The regulator is secured in the middle to a pole or at a height, that elevates above the roof of the hut in which the observation post is located". [FIG 68, p. 51]

The key to the vocabulary changed frequently to keep the system secure and its use was then dedicated to military communications during the French Revolution. Some clandestine systems were nevertheless dismantled in the years 1833–1834, while businessmen wanted access to a telecommunications network for commercial purposes. In 1837, a law was passed giving the French state a monopoly on the transmission of information by telegraph or any forthcoming means of transmission. In France, only the French government could use, manage and install the means of transmission of information for 150 years. This was known as the Post, Telegraphs and Telephones (PTT) monopoly.

The telegraph became electric, then was used with the Morse alphabet and subsequently the telephone appeared, with each change accompanied by a question that the reader must keep in mind: these forms of media made it possible to exchange information, certainly, but how to ensure the security of the information system that they support?

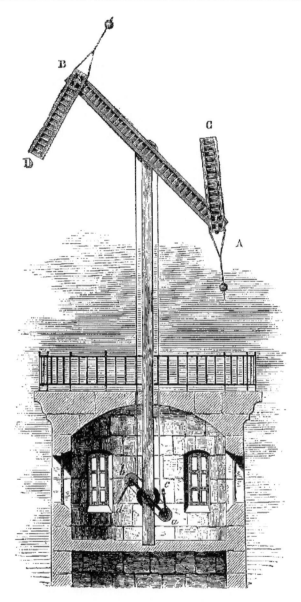

Figure 1.3. *Chappe's Telegraph (source: [FIG 68]), an artifact supporting the information system of the French State in the 19th Century*

Indeed, when governed by rigor and military discipline, the information system sees its components work according to strict and well-defined procedures. Yet, the industrial revolution went hand in hand with the liberalization of means of communication in the second half of the 19th Century. Moreover, the information system of organizations, until then confined to memoranda, account books and letters, saw the introduction of new components supported by Information and Communication Technologies. Whether it is a telegram, a telephone call, a fax or an e-mail, the question of the security of the artifacts supporting the information system arises. The question – the one which is the subject of this book – of insider threats that the employees, the human component of the information system can constitute, arises again: are they liable to spread, even unintentionally, information to someone other than its intended recipient?

In an 1878 *Instruction Manual for the Domestic Use of the Bell Telephone*, we can read that "telephones can serve to establish communications between two or several rooms in a house or any building, whether for purely domestic needs, or for commercial, industrial or administrative uses" [ROO 78, p. 1]. It becomes possible to talk remotely. The transmission time for information is reduced to the time it takes to speak the words themselves. From the point of view of information system's security, when speaking on the telephone it seems as if the natural character of this medium of transmitting information minimizes the insider threat and the risk of attacks from the human component of the information system. Indeed, unlike the torches in Polybius' system (Figure 1.1) or the Chappe brothers' telegraph (Figure 1.3), human beings naturally learn to communicate by voice. The artifact that is the telephone provides a feeling of security insofar as the interlocutor is known. Nevertheless, an attack can consist of pretending to be this interlocutor. Once again, the presence of an artifact supporting the information system leads to a false impression of security that we must be aware of. The observations that we have been able to make in the field and which are presented in the second part of this book show that independently of the object used, the human component of the information system is always susceptible to be the target of attacks.

At the end of the 19th Century, the information system integrated a human component, certainly, but also increasingly integrated components supported by artifacts, that is to say man-made products: from the Latin *arte factus* "made with art". Whether they are signals from torches, smokes signals, telegrams or telephones, these artifacts are meant to decrease the transmission time of the information within the information system. Figure 1.4 shows how the artifacts likely to support information systems in the year 2000 were envisioned in 1910.

Figure 1.4. *"Correspondence Cinéma – Phono – Télégraphique": artifacts supporting an information system in the year 2000, as seen in 1910 by Villemard (source: Bibliothèque Nationale de France)*

1.2. From the end of the 19th Century: decreasing processing time

In an information system, information is transmitted, certainly, but it is also processed. Traditional information processing techniques have evolved within organizations, particularly at the end of the 19th Century [DAN 01]. Whether they are accounting related, administrative, or commercial in nature, the quantities of information processed have become larger and larger, in fact lengthening the processing time. Managing prices, estimating and distributing costs, evaluating profits and controlling stocks are so much information processing that is likely to take a long time once large quantities of information need to be processed.

The United States Constitution of 1787 stipulated that every 10 years, a census of the nation's free people and slaves had to be taken. The young nation went from 3.9 million people at the time of the first census in 1790 to 76 million in 1900, while the length of the census reports went from 56 pages in 1790 to 26,408 pages in 1890. For each census, a new census bureau would open and then be closed after having issued its report, resulting in a lack of continuity and legibility of statistics from one census report to another [HEI 09, p. 15]. High turnover, combined with sporadic funding, led to the use of punch cards (Figure 1.5) in carrying out the 1890 census with unprecedented efficiency and precision.

Before World War I, manufacturers had begun to collect more and more information. Because businesses had been predominantly small before then, formal demand for information was almost nonexistent. Not only (1) was information accessible directly through observation, but also (2) the decisions a small business needed to make in a stable economy were relatively simple.

Starting in the 1920s, tabulating machines with punch cards were used all over the world to reduce the processing time for information [MUR 10]. The opening of new markets, national and international, as well as technological innovations, made the type of decisions managers had to make more complex, while they saw the processing of information as the source of key indicators. In addition, new systems were tested for using this information and benefitting from it in a changing economy. For Levenstein [LEV 98, p. 2]:

"Firms adopted technologies, organizational structures, and information systems to adapt to and take advantage of these new possibilities".

The demand for artifacts making it possible to process information more and more quickly came in particular from an increase in the size and number of very capitalistic businesses [LEV 98, p. 14]. The principal demand involved production rather than transactions. It entailed measuring, recording and processing what was happening internally within the business rather than in the outside world. This information was then used at different levels of the business to help decision making.

However, surviving in a competitive mass market requires a mastery of costs and margins as well as a rapid response that was adapted to client preferences and variations in the market. Thus, attention was also paid to transactions. In 1949, the British agri-food company J. Lyons was one of the first in the world to use a computer to support its information system. This business, which had no experience in electronics or computer science, designed and built the LEO I, the first stored program computer used by a private enterprise [LAN 00, p. 16].

Figure 1.5. *First page of the August 30, 1890 Scientific American showing how the artifacts supporting an information system made it possible to reduce processing time*

Despite a large number of daily transactions, Lyons was making an extremely low average profit, around a fraction of a penny [LAN 00, p. 17]. In 1923, the top management decided to recruit John Simmons, a statistician, who would later say:

> "In fact I was engaged to try to build up a system of information for the management of the company which would be superior, more sensible, than just depending upon the profit and loss account and such like [...] in this respect the company was already ahead". [CAM 98, Annex B, pp. 360–374]

Simmons had risen through the ranks and set up the Systems Research Office whose job was evaluating existing systems, traveling the world in search of better ways to support management activities and inventing, testing and implementing improvements. Numerous innovations have, moreover, been set up by the Systems Research Office, in particular the concept of "sales representatives", each one with responsibility for a small group of retailers with a duty of accounting, credit, payment, etc.

Over the years, Lyons developed a new management style where information went from operations, manufacturing, sales and distribution to bills and payments. Each subsidiary of the business had its managers who reported on its activity. These masses of information were summarized and compared in relation to standards, forecasts and budgets. It was thus possible for the management to inquire about the effect of a 10% reduction in the production of chocolate, for example, on overall profit.

In 1947, two of the company's top executives visited the United States to see the changes in office equipment since the end of Second World War. There was nothing new, except that they heard about an "electronic brain", the Engineering Numerical Integrator And Computer (ENIAC), used by the army and for engineering calculations. They very quickly grasped the possibilities of this type of equipment for economic and commercial calculations and they began to visit the pioneers who were using the installation. Significantly, at Harvard and Princeton they learned that Cambridge University in England was in the process of developing an Electronic Delay Storage Automatic Calculator (EDSAC). Returning to England, the two men visited Cambridge, where they noticed that the development of the machine was very slow. They made a report to Simmons, which included the following:

> "Here, for the first time, there is a possibility of a machine which will be able to cope, at almost incredible speed, with any variation of clerical procedures, provided the conditions which govern the variations is predetermined. What effect such machines could have on the semi repetitive work of the office needs only the slightest effort of imagination. The possible savings from such a machine should be at least £50,000 a year. The capital cost would be of the order of £100,000" [LAN 00, p. 19].

In this report, they also proposed building a machine in Lyons' workshops based on the university's advice. In 1949, Lyons agreed to financially support Cambridge University once it had shown the EDSAC's ability to solve complicated mathematical problems. In exchange, the university would help Lyons create its own computer, the Lyons Electronic Office (LEO). In 1951, the LEO team created the basis of the computer whose first applications would concern the bakeries of Lyons. In 1953, the LEO I (Figure 1.6) was formally declared operational [LAN 00, p. 20].

Figure 1.6. *Control console of the LEO I in 1953 (source: the LEO Computers Society). For the first time, a computer system supported an information system in a business*

The first mass-produced computer was the IBM 650, produced between 1954 and 1962. In 1957, the Railway Technical Research Institute imported the first stored program computer to Japan, a Bendix G-15, to conduct research on seat reservation systems [MUR 10]. During Japan's 1955–1973 period of high growth, the development and the use of information systems supported by computers made it possible to streamline business procedures and to reduce costs [MUR 10, p. 5]. By 1961 in Japan, the number of orders for computers had surpassed orders for punch card systems.

In 1968, in front of a crowd of around 1,000 professionals and researchers in computer science, Douglas Engelbart of the Augmentation Research Center of the Stanford Research Institute in California demonstrated a computer system, hardware and software, which he and his team had been working on since 1962. For the first time, two people located in different places could share a screen and work simultaneously on a file while communicating through a network with an audio and video interface. It also involved the first use of a mouse and hypertext links. Figure 1.7 shows this system's interface and corresponds to an extract of the recording of the 1968 demonstration. Computer systems then would gradually support the information systems within organizations. In fact, not only did they considerably increase the processing time of information, but they also made it possible to transmit different types of information (text, audio and video). Information transmission and processing times were reduced even more and confusion was created between "computer system" and "information system". However, although the first is confined to processing information automatically, the second integrates a human component that must not be forgotten. The increase in quantities of information to be processed brought about the use of computer systems to support the information system. Paradoxically, computer systems, although they have allowed the transmission and processing of information at a high speed, have at the same time considerably massified the quantities of information to be transmitted and processed.

Figure 1.7. *Audio and video interface with screen sharing in 1968 (source: web.stanford.edu); confusion developed between "computer system" and "information system"*

1.3. From the end of the 20th Century: facing massification

The reader might be surprised to discover the contents of the previous section: if people were already sharing screens remotely and exchanging audio and video information through a computer system within an information system in 1968, what happened after that? Close to half a century after Engelbart's demonstration, the information system seems to be supported by the same type of artifacts (computer systems) with the same goals (decreasing information transmission and processing times). This is the case. Nevertheless, the change is not any less tangible than that of the massification of the information to be transmitted and processed.

By way of illustration, Figure 1.8(a) shows the ARPANET (Advanced Research Projects Agency Network) in 1977; this network would serve as the basis of the Internet and connected major universities in the United States as well as the Pentagon. Figure 1.8(b) presents the Internet network in 2015, where each line corresponds to an exchange of information between two IP addresses. These figures show the massive change in the amount of information exchanged through the network between 1977 and 2015.

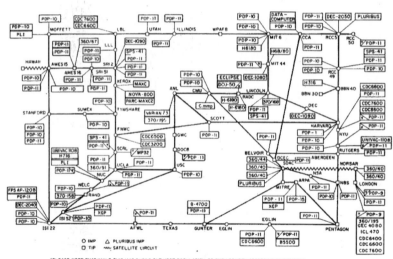

a)

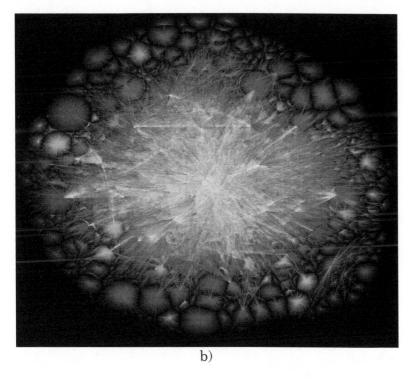

b)

Figure 1.8. *a) The ARPANET in 1977 and b) the Internet in 2015*

This evolution goes hand in hand with the uses that are made of the digital artifacts supporting the information systems within organizations. For authors such as Bryant [BRY 08]: "IS [...] is inevitably caught up in an ambivalent relationship with modernity". Where an executive could use a telephone in 1930, today all of the employees have access to the outside world from their work stations, whether through the business' information system or through their own means. They also represent a threat to the information system's security from within the organization itself: they represent an *insider threat*.

2

Components with Interpretive Aspects: People

We are constantly interacting with the world that surrounds us through a filter. The information that we perceive is filtered and we create knowledge that is specific to us. Work we did in the past leads us to create metrics that make it possible to determine to what extent two individuals give the same meaning to the same information [ARD 13]. In fact, this indescribable filter through which we perceive the world is called an interpretative framework [TSU 93]. Some talk about mental models [JON 11] or even "neural apparatus", [KUH 70] making the interpretative framework a complex piece of machinery, a place of chemical reactions that can be analyzed. Others believe that above all it involves the socioindividual [YAM 10], which results from our history, a place for expressing a form of intellectual creativity that is specific to each person.

Thus, we all act as agents interpreting through this filter that allows us to create knowledge that is specific to us from information that we collect; knowledge which is likely to vary from one person to another. Even as this work was undertaken, a large taboo was that of philosophy. What is knowledge? How do we perceive the world around us? These are examples of some questions which we are not going to elaborate on, but will well and truly respond to from the point of view of the organization. Since it is there that the research materials that we will work with are found: individuals, their knowledge and their interpretative frameworks.

This chapter consists of four sections: section 2.1 presents Polanyi's concept of *tacit knowing*, a fully developed concept that nevertheless does not specify the existence of this filter, the interpretative framework, which was introduced by S. Tsuchiya and is addressed in section 2.2. Section 2.3 (re)updates incommensurability as T.S. Kuhn proposed it in the 1970s. It is the principal cause, or consequence, of communication breakdowns. Section 2.4 discusses mental models and the way in which they can be assimilated into interpretative frameworks.

2.1. Tacit knowing or, how do we know?

In 1967, Polanyi was interested above all in the way in which we endow our discourse with meaning (by speaking or by writing, for example) and in what we attribute meaning to (by listening or by reading, for example). Although they are informal, these actions possess a characteristic model that Polanyi [POL 67] calls the structure of tacit knowing:

> "Both the way we endow our own utterances with meaning and our attribution of meaning to the utterances of others are acts of tacit knowing. They represent sense-giving and sense-reading within the structure of tacit knowing". [POL 67, p. 301]

2.1.1. *The existence of tacit knowledge*

Back in the 1960s, every morning at breakfast Polanyi read his letters in several languages. One morning he saw his son come in, and wanted to pass a letter on to him. Remembering that his son only spoke English, he checked the letter and realized that it was in a foreign language. Polanyi was therefore conscious of the meaning conveyed by the letter but not the worlds that had conveyed it. He then explained the contents of the letter to his son in English. This clearly shows that one can (1) possess the meaning of a text without knowing the text itself and (2) put this inarticulate meaning into words [POL 67].

We can therefore possess unarticulated knowledge which Polanyi calls tacit knowledge.

Polanyi has insisted since 1967 that: "[...] modern positivism has tried to ignore it, on the grounds that tacit knowledge was not accessible to objective observation" [POL 67]. As a temporary difficulty, the fact that language is nothing until there is knowledge of its meaning was ignored at the time and that still seems to be the case today. There has been extremely large economic investment in information technologies and collaborative tools since the 1970s. Yet, as Landauer [LAN 95] remarked, the productivity of these services that have been invested in is stagnating throughout the world.

2.1.2. Sense-giving and sense-reading: knowledge is tacit

The retranscription of the letter that Polanyi offered his son was that of the meaning of the letter as he understood it. Imagine that the letter describes a scene that the sender, a traveler, wrote it while he witnessed it. Maybe he admired a landscape, a particular instance of trees, fields, rivers and mountains. When he reported on the scene, he used the general terms "trees", "fields", "rivers" and "mountains", which do not transmit the particular instance that he has witnessed. In doing so, by choosing the words to describe his experience, he has performed a *sense-giving action* [POL 67];

he has endowed them with meaning for himself (Figure 2.1). His lived experience, his perceptions and his tacit knowledge of the place he visited have thus been communicated in the form of knowledge made explicit a letter, whose meaning was tacit.

In receiving the letter and reading it, Polanyi perceives shapes and colors, from which he understands words. Once perceived, the word is forgotten to give way to the meaning attributed to it, which corresponds to a *sense-reading* action [POL 67] (Figure 2.1). He is therefore conscious of the meaning of the letter without remembering the text, which is why he forgot that his son, who only spoke English, could not read it.

By communicating his lived experience in a letter, the sender gives meaning to the words, knowledge made explicit whose meaning is tacit: "[...] into a communication which was a piece of explicit knowledge, the meaning of which was tacit. All knowledge falls into one of these two classes: it is either *tacit* or *rooted in tacit knowledge*" [POL 67, p. 314]. In this way, all knowledge is either tacit or rooted in tacit knowledge.

Polanyi heavily insists on the "contradiction" of the existence of knowledge made explicit, since, without their tacit coefficients, all words, all formulas, all maps and all images are simply devoid of meaning. The example that he uses is that of the cyclist who at any time is offsetting their imbalance by turning the bicycle in a curve with a radius proportional to the square root of its speed, divided by the angle of their imbalance. This rule, although made explicit, is useless in learning how to ride a bicycle. Moreover, for someone who does not grasp its tacit meaning, it is not understood (Figure 2.2).

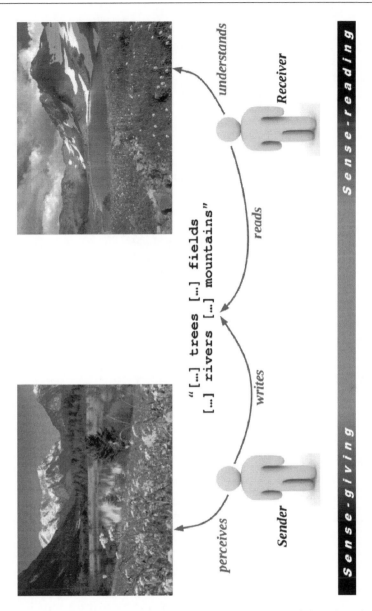

Figure 2.1. *Sense-giving and sense-reading constitute tacit knowing, the basic structure of the knowledge transfer. For a color version of the figure, see www.iste.co.uk/arduin/insider.zip*

Figure 2.2. *Knowledge is tacit: this formula, although explicit, is useless for the cyclist. Moreover, for someone who does not grasp its meaning, which is tacit, this remains uncomprehended*

Polanyi [POL 67] presents another telling example, this time that of a young radiology intern. Beginning by observing a radiologist comment on shadows on X-rays in technical language to his assistants, he is helpless to distinguish the bones on the X-rays at best. As he listens, while looking carefully at the images in different cases, a panorama of significant details will be revealed to him. The images will gradually make sense to him as well as the comments that are associated with them. Polanyi is talking about the "educational expansion of the mind" but – as we will see – it is the increase in the commensurability of the interpretative frameworks, which is questioned here.

2.2. The interpretative framework, the filter through which we create our knowledge

Based on the concepts of *sense-giving* and *sense-reading* proposed by Polanyi, S. Tsuchiya introduced the idea of the interpretative framework. Specific to each person, the interpretative framework is one of the elements that allows sense-giving and sense-reading actions to operate:

> "When   datum   is   sense-given   through interpretative framework, it becomes information, and when information is sense-read through interpretative framework, it becomes knowledge" [TSU 93, p. 88]

2.2.1. *A tool for tacit knowing*

We constantly adopt what is not under our control and what is found in the world that surrounds us: information. Information is transmitted by talking, writing or action during a sense-giving process. We collect data from this information by listening, reading or watching during a sense-reading process. When he studied the concepts of sense-giving and sense-reading, Tsuchiya [TSU 93] highlighted the idea that knowledge was the result of the interpretation of information by an individual. These processes activate the relevant interpretative frameworks as well as preexisting knowledge depending on the context, the situation and our intention. Possibly, new tacit knowledge is created (see [GRU 12] on this subject).

As the author of this document, I possess tacit knowledge that I have structured into information during a sense-giving process. As a reader of this document, you have interpreted this information by perceiving shapes and colors, integrated words and data during a sense-reading process and potentially created new tacit knowledge (see Figure 2.3).

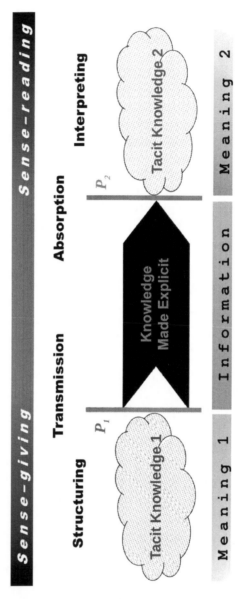

Figure 2.3. *The transfer of tacit knowledge. For a color version of the figure, see www.iste.co.uk/arduin/insider.zip*

When a person P_1 structures his/her tacit knowledge and transmits it, he/she creates knowledge made explicit, information created from his/her tacit knowledge. A person P_2 perceiving this information and absorbing it, potentially creates new tacit knowledge for him/herself.

Knowledge is the result of the interpretation by an individual of information.

This interpretation is done through an interpretative framework that filters the data contained in the information and with the use of preexisting tacit knowledge as presented by Tsuchiya [TSU 93].

Knowledge results from the interpretation of information by an individual. This interpretation leads to the creation of meaning that can vary from one individual to another: this is *meaning variance* [ARD 14, ARD 15]. Diffusing information does not necessarily imply a transfer of knowledge. Arduin [ARD 13] has proposed metrics for determining to what extent two individuals will, starting from the same piece of information, create the same knowledge.

This question of "meaning variance" is central in organizations, although too hidden and too indirectly addressed. The intangible character of knowledge is often a hindrance to its consideration. Nevertheless, knowledge is a resource that can be characterized as crucial when it is necessary for carrying out the business' activities [GRU 05]. While certain authors such as Liebowitz [LIE 08] offer methodologies to ensure the continued existence of knowledge, others such as Nonaka and Konno [NON 98] set up places for exchange to facilitate its creation and sharing. Some authors even talk about "immaterial assets" whose value could be measured [BOU 06].

2.2.2. *The different types of interpretative frameworks*

According to S. Tsuchiya, interpretative frameworks can be characterized as those following four different modes by using two key dimensions [TSU 93, TSU 99]. He references Daft and Weick [DAF 84] who proposed studying the way in which organizations interpret their environment. They already thought that "interpretation gives meaning to data" (p. 286) and S. Tsuchiya thus proposes drawing a parallel between organizational interpretation and individual interpretation.

The model defined by R.L. Daft and K.E. Weick provides a means of describing and explaining the way in which knowledge about an environment is obtained. It revolves around two dimensions:

1) belief in the analyzability of the environment;

2) intrusion into the environment in order to understand it.

2.2.2.1. *Belief in the analyzability of the environment*

To explain this dimension, the authors introduce the game known as Twenty Questions: one person leaves the room and during this time the group chooses a word. After returning, the person must guess the word by asking 20 questions whose response can only be yes or no.

A variant of this game was proposed in 1967 by the physicist J.A. Wheeler [WHE 67]. The group no longer chooses a word, each one deciding to respond yes or no as he hears it, all the while taking into account previous responses. Gradually, a response corresponding to all of the questions has been created by the group.

For R.L. Daft and K.E. Weick, we are constantly playing these games by testing and questioning the environment to get responses. The difference between one or the other of the games reflects whether or not we believe that the environment is analyzable, that is to say if the responses already exist in it or not. If the environment is perceived as somewhat changeable, it is possible that we would consider it less analyzable.

2.2.2.2. Intrusion into the environment in order to understand it

If the environment in which we find ourselves seems hostile, or if we greatly depend on it, we will deploy more resources and be more intrusive, Weick and Daft [WEI 83] talk about "test-makers". On the contrary, we can be content to interpret within the accepted limits and then be "test-avoiders" [WEI 79].

Thus, S. Tsuchiya relies on these authors and their *"interpretation behaviors"* [DAF 84, p. 287] in order to create the four types of interpretative frameworks (see Figure 2.4):

1) a passive approach hypothesizing a non-analyzable environment is characterized as being *undirected viewing*. We do not rely on raw data since the environment is considered non-analyzable and we act on limited and imprecise information to create our perception of the environment;

2) an equally passive approach, but one hypothesizing an analyzable environment, is characterized as *conditioned viewing*. The interpretations do not rest on precise data but they are made within traditional borders. It is conditioned insofar as the meanings that it creates are limited to the routine (documents, reports, information systems that are already old, etc.);

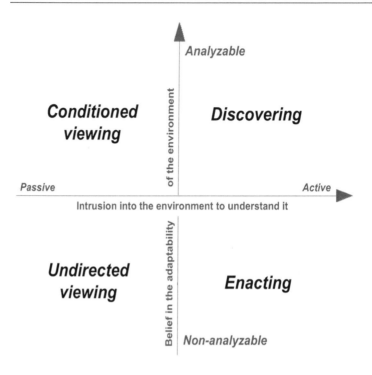

Figure 2.4. *The different types of interpretative frameworks:*
intrusion or non-intrusion into the environment,
which is judged analyzable or non-analyzable

3) an intrusive approach with the hypothesis of an analyzable environment is characterized as *discovering*. We try to discover responses already present in an analyzable environment. Studies and measurements are conceived and these are formal data which determine the interpretations;

4) finally, an equally intrusive approach but one with the hypothesis of a non-analyzable environment is characterized as *enacting*. We construct our own environment. We try new behaviors and observe what happens. We experiment, we test and we simulate. We ignore any previous rules and traditional expectations.

In the articles cited above, R.L. Daft and K.E. Weick propose very precise analyses of the links between the mode of interpretation and the functioning of the organization.

2.2.3. *The commensurability of interpretative frameworks*

In introducing interpretative frameworks, Tsuchiya [TSU 93] concretized Polanyi's tacit knowing [POL 67]. He shaped that which we have all already observed at least once: it happens that two people understand the same piece of information differently. This created knowledge has not been the same as discussed and measured by Arduin [ARD 13].

Kuhn [KUH 70] was the first to consider commensurability as a sort of "cognitive compatibility" of concepts, problems, facts and assertions. In [MUR 92], commensurability is a type of "common denominator" for interpretative frameworks.

The choice of the term "commensurable" for comparing interpretative frameworks is not justified by Tsuchiya [TSU 93]. Nevertheless, when Kuhn [KUH 70] introduced the concept of incommensurability he insisted on its difference from incomparability in particular: theories which can never communicate with each other, which can never make the other change point of view are incomparable (see [KUH 70] on this subject). Hence this choice of "incommensurability", a term which carries a certain plasticity that each one of us has: the capacity to change points of view, to transcend ourselves, to spread out the commensurability of our interpretative frameworks.

Thus, when the probability that the same information will be interpreted by two individuals in the same way is high, we say that their interpretative frameworks have a strong commensurability or are commensurable (Figure 2.5(a)).

Conversely, when this probability is low, we say that their interpretative frameworks have a low commensurability or are incommensurable (Figure 2.5(b)). Until Arduin [ARD 13], most of the scientific community seemed to be satisfied with this more or less precise rule and whose application in the field remains specious. Arduin [ARD 14, ARD 15] proposes to study, predict and measure *meaning variance*.

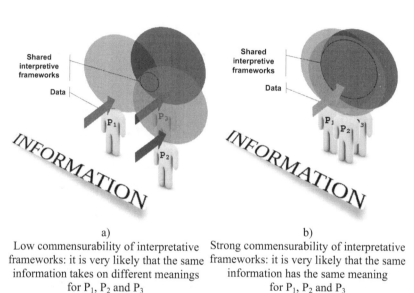

a)
Low commensurability of interpretative frameworks: it is very likely that the same information takes on different meanings for P_1, P_2 and P_3

b)
Strong commensurability of interpretative frameworks: it is very likely that the same information has the same meaning for P_1, P_2 and P_3

Figure 2.5. *a) Weak and b) strong commensurability of interpretative frameworks*

2.3. The concept of incommensurability

In mathematics, two non-null real numbers a and b are commensurable if and only if there exists a unit u of which a and b are common multiples, in other words, if and only if there exists a pair of integers (m, n) such as $a = mu$ and $b = nu$. Thus, "a and b are commensurable" and "a/b is a rational number" are two equivalent properties; there exists a common measurement between a and b (see Figure 2.6).

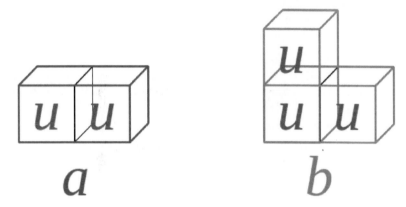

Figure 2.6. *Commensurability in mathematics: here a = 2u and b = 3u, a/b = 2/3 is a rational number, a and b are therefore commensurable*

This definition of commensurability/incommensurability goes back to antiquity and has today been replaced with the concept of the rational number. Kuhn [KUH 70], as a historian and philosopher of science, reintroduces the term "incommensurable" to describe theories whose meanings differ in a "subtle" way.

2.3.1. *From partial communication to incommensurability*

Kuhn [KUH 70] introduces his remarks by imagining his readers: according to him they are divided into two groups. The partial or incomplete communication that is established between the members of these two groups is the origin of a form of "*communication breakdown*" [KUH 70]. This type of communication that he also calls "*talking-through-each-other*" regularly characterizes a discussion between people with incommensurable points of view.

He talks about partial communication because he believes that it can be improved, unlike his contemporaries such as P.K. Feyerabend who talks about incommensurability [KUH 70], or K. Popper who thinks that "we are prisoners attached to the models of our theories; to our expectations; our past experiences; our language" [POP 63]. We could therefore, for T.S. Kuhn, "break out" of our framework at any time to move to another that is "better and roomier" and which we could also break out of at any moment.

In order to compare two successive theories, a neutral intermediary language is necessary and, from the end of the 17th Century, philosophers established the existence of such a language. A great deal of research then began attempting to express every language in a single one. A language which would be made up of a primitive vocabulary, of words conveying pure and sense data (that is to say, which make sense), and syntactic connectors. Today philosophers have abandoned the quest for this ideal. P.K. Feyerabend and T.S. Kuhn believe that it does not exist inasmuch as the passage from one theory to another changes its meaning or its conditions for applicability "in subtle ways". We can continue to use the same signs ("force", "mass", "element", etc.), but the way in which they are linked to nature, which is to say their meaning, may have changed. Such theories are for them incommensurable. Thus, two theories are called incommensurables when their meanings or conditions for applicability differ subtly.

The choice of the term "incommensurability" is justified by T.S. Kuhn who believes that the possibility of a change in points of view must be taken into account, thus abandoning the rigidity of the term "incomparability", which does not entail any change. I. Lakatos had moreover reproached him about this choice by asking him to talk about "semantic reinterpretations", a formulation which seems in sync with the Web 3.0, the semantic Web.

2.3.2. Language – linking words to nature

T.S. Kuhn poses the question: why is translation so complicated? According to him, it is because languages carve up the world in different ways and because we do not have access to neutral sublinguistic means. A good translation manual should thus always be accompanied by paragraphs explaining how those for whom it is a native language see the world. Learning to translate a language or a theory is learning to describe the world with which the language or the theory works. A dictionary will teach us what the words mean. By studying these words, we learn more, and from other words encountered in phrases, we learn all that we know. We learn by pairing words or phrases and nature. Our knowledge of the world is embodied in the mechanism, which has been used for linking words to nature.

These are the "essences" that populate the Aristotelian universe (Figure 2.7), while "chemical elements" occupy Mendeleev's periodic table of elements (Figure 2.8). To what extent do we endow these representations their original meanings today?

Figure 2.7. *A representation of the solar system according to Aristotle, extract from the Cosmographicus liber of Petrus Apianus in 1524*

ОПЫТЪ СИСТЕМЫ ЭЛЕМЕНТОВЪ.

ОСНОВАННОЙ НА ИХЪ АТОМНОМЪ ВѢСѢ И ХИМИЧЕСКОМЪ СХОДСТѢ.

```
                        Ti = 50    Zr = 90      ? = 180.
                         V = 51    Nb = 94     Ta = 182.
                        Cr = 52    Mo = 96      W = 186.
                        Mn = 55    Rh = 104,4  Pt = 197,4.
                        Fe = 56    Rn = 104,4   Ir = 198.
                   Ni = Co = 59    Pl = 106,8   O- = 199.
  H = 1                 Cu = 63,4  Ag = 108    Hg = 200.
          Be = 9,4 Mg = 24  Zn = 65,2  Cd = 112
          B = 11    Al = 27,4   ? = 68  Ur = 116   Au = 197?
          C = 12    Si = 28     ? = 70  Sn = 118
          N = 14     P = 31   As = 75   Sb = 122   Bi = 210?
          O = 16     S = 32   Se = 79,4 Te = 128?
          F = 19    Cl = 35,5 Br = 80    I = 127
  Li = 7 Na = 23     K = 39   Rb = 85,4 Cs = 133  Tl = 204.
                    Ca = 40   Sr = 87,6 Ba = 137  Pb = 207.
                     ? = 45   Ce = 92
                   ?Er = 56   La = 94
                   ?Yt = 60   Di = 95
                   ?In = 75,6 Th = 118?
```

Д. Менделѣевъ

Figure 2.8. *Mendeleev's table, the periodic classification of elements, in 1869*

2.3.3. *Revolution – changing the meaning of words*

Human beings are verbal creatures. We have all learned a language that, for us, links words to nature and to the world that surrounds us. This language is infused with our own way of seeing the world. This is the same mechanism which makes, for example, specialists interpret Newton's Second Law $f = ma$, which becomes $mg = \frac{md^{2}s}{dt^{2}}$ for a free fall, or $mg\sin\theta = -ml\frac{d^{2}\theta}{dt^{2}}$ for a pendulum, while for harmonic oscillations it involves two equations among others: $m_1\frac{d^{2}s_1}{dt^{2}} + k_1s_1 = k_2(d + s_2 - s_1)$, etc. Thus, even this law of physics has different interpretations.

Language, whether it is natural or scientific, can be interpreted differently.

In [KUH 70, p. 276], the sources of communication breakdown are extraordinarily difficult to isolate and get past. Two men, even if they are looking at the same thing, even if they have the same data, can arrive at different interpretations. A communication breakdown is likely to prove that these two men can see different things or rather see the same thing differently. Their *neural apparatus* [KUH 70, p. 276] can be programmed differently (see Figure 2.9). The variation between what is in nature and what they perceive as being in nature is correlated to the corresponding variation in the language-nature interaction. The individuals share a history (except the immediate past), a language, an everyday environment, etc. and should have, according to T.S. Kuhn, a neural apparatus programmed in the same way. Given what they share, they can better understand how they differ.

Figure 2.9. *A communication breakdown: the two people link terms to nature differently. For example here when A ≠ B*

Above all, when they experience a communication breakdown, the two men can discover the place where it originates through experimentation. Often the center of the difficulty involves ambiguous terms such as "element" or "component", which the two men use without a problem but which we can now see interact with nature differently. For each one of the terms, there exist others in a basic vocabulary and which do not create any discussion, request for explanation or disagreement if they are used intragroup. If they find that these terms are a source of special difficulties for the intergroup discussion, our men can access their shared vocabularies of daily life to clarify these problems. With time, T.S. Kuhn assures that they will become great predictors of each other's behavior. In the process, he proposed, starting in 1970, pathways to limiting communication breakdowns, to facilitate *tacit knowing* and to increase the commensurability of interpretative frameworks.

2.4. Mental models, representations of reality

An interpretative framework, as we have seen, is a filter through which we select data that we have collected from information. We interpret these data, allowing us to create knowledge.

An analogy can be made here with mental models, which are defined by Jones *et al.* [JON 11] as follows:

> "Mental models are internal and personal representations of external reality used by individuals to interact with the world that surrounds them. [...] They provide the mechanism through which new information is filtered and recorded".

Jones *et al.* [JON 11] do not hesitate to underline the benefits in considering the plurality of perceptions: "Recognizing and dealing with the plurality of stakeholder's perceptions, values, and goals is currently considered a key aspect of effective [...] management practice".

2.4.1. *Incomplete representations*

In cognitive science, as in psychology, it is accepted that individuals use internal representations of external reality to interact with the world (on this subject, see [CRA 43], who was one of the first to draw a parallel between the functioning of machines and the human brain). These are mental models. They are considered cognitive structures at the root of reasoning, decision-making and behavior (see Figure 2.10).

Individuals build their mental models from their personal experiences, their perceptions and their understandings of the world. This involves incomplete representations of reality that are also inconsistent since they depend on context and can change depending on the situation in which they are used. The term "incomplete" is therefore not to be understood in the mathematical sense of "completeness" but rather in the sense of an abstraction that eliminates the details of reality, which are not relevant in the given context and situation.

Various tools and techniques have been developed to gain insight into the internal representations that an individual may have. We can especially consider of the field of organizational research with Hall [HAL 94] and his cognitive maps, or Morgan [MOR 02] and his studies on risk in communication.

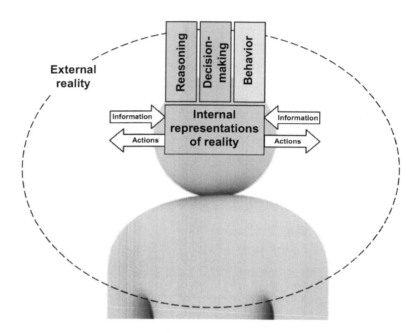

Figure 2.10. *Mental models are internal representations of external reality at the root of reasoning, decision-making and behavior*

Thus, a mental model is a somewhat functional representation of reality [JON 11]. Simplified, inexact and incomplete, this representation is influenced by the person's goals and motivations, as well as by his or her preexisting knowledge [JON 11, p. 5]. With the theory of *confirmation bias*, Klayman and Ha [KLA 89] suggest that individuals seek out information adapted to their understanding of the world. Mental models play a role in the filtering of information. Morgan [MOR 02] is interested, for example, in the means of spreading information in forms compatible with the understanding of those to whom it is addressed.

2.4.2. Cognitive representations

Once again it was Craik [CRA 43] who first proposed that people carry in their minds a small-scale model of how the world works. According to Collins and Gentner [COL 87], mental models are formed by analogy. When a person explains an area that is not familiar to him/her, they tend to use an example from a familiar domain that they perceives as being similar: they copies an existing mental model whose relational structure they import. For example, we can use the flow of water to explain electrical currents (see Figure 2.11). Studies by Rickheit and Sichelschmidt [RIC 99] show that when a phenomenon cannot be perceived directly, individuals often explain it in this way.

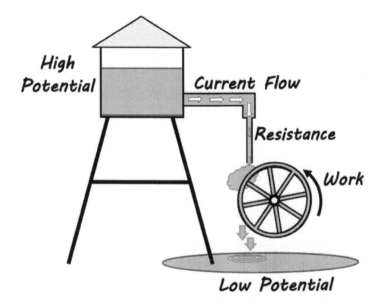

Figure 2.11. *Using the flow of water to explain electrical currents, an example of copying an existing mental model to explain an unknown domain*

In [ABE 98], it is by creating a cognitive map that individuals acquire, code and recall information about the world. Creating a cognitive map is a process that "enables people to generalize on the basis of past experiences and to use these generalizations (or generic information) in other contexts" [DOW 76, p. 69]. According to Kearney and Kaplan [KER 97], cognitive maps are structures of knowledge representing an individual's hypotheses, beliefs and false ideas about the world. These hypotheses and beliefs provide a framework to interpret new information and to determine appropriate responses to new situations [KAP 82, KAP 89].

2.4.3. *Shared mental models*

The field of cognitive anthropology, which is interested in the "way in which cultural knowledge is organized within the mind" [D'AN 95, p. 279], studies culture at the cognitive level. Anthropologists talk about "schema", which Quinn [QUI 05] defines as being "a generic version of (some part of) the world built up from experience and stored in memory" [QUI 05, p. 38]. The "cultural schema" is developed through shared experiences [QUI 05, p. 38] and over time, as the members of a group internalize their shared experiences, cultural meaning is created. Individuals use it to perceive the world around them [QUI 05].

These studies on cultural mental models concern the degree of comprehension shared among a group of individuals. Langan-Fox *et al.* [LAN 00] discussed the idea that "effective team functioning requires the existence of a shared or team mental model among members of a team" [LAN 00, p. 242]. This idea has led organizational research to look more attentively at the study of mental models: the existence of a mental model shared between the members of a team being necessary to ensure it functions effectively. A shared mental model is a mental model created and shared by individuals who interact together in a group [LAN 01].

Improving the decision-making process requires encouraging individuals who have different points of view to work together. A shared comprehension among the different involved parties must be identified and supported [JON 11]. With decision-making involving the individual, the group, and society all at the same time, research on mental models no longer concentrates only on the individual, but also on the collective. There is a social component in cognition, awareness of what is necessary to understand the insider threat.

Here, a link with interpretative frameworks begins to be detectable and should not be neglected: the shared mental model, a mental model constructed and shared among individuals who interact together in a group, makes one think of a strong commensurability of interpretative frameworks (see Figure 2.5(b)). It is very likely that the same information will be interpreted in the same way by the members of a group possessing a shared mental model. In other words, the commensurability of their interpretative frameworks is strong in the sense that the number of their common interpretative frameworks is large. The *same* information will be a source of the *same* knowledge for the members of this group. This analogy has never been made in the literature and can open up new avenues of investigation into interpretative frameworks, in particular in relation to the study of methodologies for making mental models explicit.

2.4.4. *Explaining mental models*

Jones *et al.* [JON 11] present different ways of making mental models explicit. For them, mental models can be made explicit for the following reasons:

– to study the similarities and differences in comprehension between different individuals and to improve communication;

– to improve the overall comprehension of a system;

– to create a collective representation of a system in order to improve the decision-making process;

– to support social learning processes;

– to identify and fight the limitations of individuals' knowledge;

– to develop more socially robust knowledge to support negotiations.

The majority of the procedures used to make mental models explicit begin with the hypothesis that they can be represented as a network of concepts and relationships. Some make a representation explicit in the form of a network directly from an interview. Others require the researcher to recreate or interfere with the network by working from an interview or with the help of a questionnaire.

2.4.4.1. *Direct explanation*

Here, the interviewee is asked to create a representation of his or her mental model in the form of a diagram using drawings, words and symbols. Kearney and Kaplan [KEA 97] mention for example the *"Conceptual Content Cognitive Map (3CM)"*, a method where the participants must identify the concepts that they consider important for a given domain. They are then asked to organize the concepts visually/ spatially in a way that represents their understanding of this domain. This method is inspired by "wayfinding" techniques in which researchers are interested in the way in which people perceive a geographical environment that asks them to make drawings of this region. These drawings are then used to evaluate the cognitive maps of this area for each individual. For Kearney and Kaplan [KEA 97], this exercise is extremely compatible with the way in which humans process information: cognition being not only based on language, but also on images. On the contrary, Furth

[FUR 71] has shown through studies on the thought processes of deaf children that cognition is not based on language. Moreover, words and concepts can only be associated linguistically, linguistic structure not being synonymous with cognitive structure: we can link "cat" to "hat" and "capital" without these words being connected semantically. Insofar as these limits are felt, Kearney and Kaplan [KEA 97] highlight the responses provided by the 3CM method and discuss this method's conceptual validity. Conceptual validity corresponds to the degree in which a measurement technique evaluates what it is supposed to evaluate. We believe that there is strong validity when (1) the measurement works according to theoretical expectations and (2) the measurement shows expected behaviors vis-à-vis other measurements. Two implementations of 3CM exist: open-ended implementation, which is adapted to small samples, and structured implementation, which requires 15–25 min on average no matter the number of participants.

– *Open-ended implementation*: After having introduced a particular domain to the participants, we ask them to think about the way in which they would explain their own vision of this domain to someone unfamiliar with it. They then list the aspects of this domain that seem important to them. After writing each one on a card, the cards are placed facing them. When they think they have listed everything, we ask them to group the cards together and arrange them in a way that illustrates how they perceive this domain. Equivalence classes are created as the participants believe that concepts can be grouped together. In doing so, we have built cognitive maps for each one of them.

– *Structured implementation*: A list of concepts encompassing the whole domain is first generated (by a survey of a representative group rather than by a group of experts in order to ensure a good understanding of these concepts by all of the participants, or through the use of an open-ended implementation of 3CM). All of these concepts are then presented to each participant with a scenario. We then ask them to think about the way in which they would explain their vision of this domain to a friend who is unfamiliar with it. They must then choose concepts that seem important to them to explain their vision of the domain. When appropriate, they are invited to add concepts that do not appear in the proposed group. Finally, they are asked to organize these concepts into groups according to how well they believe the concepts go together and to give a name to each group.

The data resulting from 3CM studies can be studied through multidimensional analysis techniques and compiled in similarity matrices. A similarity matrix is a *Concept* × *Concept* matrix where each entry ij represents the percentage of participants who grouped concept i together with concept j. In this way, the method combines qualitative and quantitative procedures in order to determine the similarities and differences in the understanding of the participants. The attention that is paid to objects that the participants have provides the 3CM method with a certain precision in its analysis of knowledge structures. It proposes to identify the concepts seen as important by each person and to organize them.

Ozesmi and Ozesmi [OZE 04] have proposed a similar approach: they create mental models by asking interviewees to define the important variables of a given system. These variables are then written on cards and the participants must organize them in a way that reflects their understanding of the system. This approach elucidates the causal comprehension of a system and thus aims at the links from cause to effect between the concepts. Tools from graph theory are then used to explore the complexity of networks, their density, the number of links, how frequently the variables appear, etc. To quote Ozesmi and Ozesmi [OZE 04]: "By examining the structure of maps we can determine how stakeholders view the system, for example whether they perceive a lot of forcing functions affecting the system which are out of their control, or whether they see the system as hierarchical or more democratic" (p. 50). For them, this form of participative model is preferable when (1) the scientific data or experts are limited, uncertain or unavailable and (2) when the support of stakeholders is necessary, the "locals" then play a key role in the construction of the model. The interested reader can consult the articles [DRA 06, DRA 07] where a similar approach is used to build a collective representation through a role-playing game. The game becoming a support for negotiation and decision-making. Through interaction, the participants are capable of exploring and comparing their mental models.

Participative models using explanation techniques of mental models in order to create a collective representation or a shared mental model are notably used to support collective decision-making [LYN 02]. The ARDI method: *Actors Resources, Dynamics and Interaction* [ETI 11, MAT 11] is one example. It involves systematically asking participants what, according to them, are the key actors and resources, the processes and dynamics in a system as well as their interactions. This exercise creates an influence diagram, a representation of an individual or group mental model that can be used as a support tool for the dialogue [JON 11].

2.4.4.2. *Indirect explanation*

In [CAR 92], the representation of a mental model can be extracted from written documents or oral text, verbal structure being an example of a symbolic representation of an individual's cognitive structure. The motivations of these studies are often differences in comprehension encumbering communication and cooperation, as is the case when the commensurability of interpretative frameworks is low. Mixed open and semistructured discussions can allow for the exploration of the similarities and differences in comprehension between the members of a group [ABE 98].

Consensus analysis is an approach to making mental models explicit that does not have the goal of representing them as a network of concepts and relationships, but which rather aims at studying the distribution of cultural knowledge in a group of individuals [STO 11]. Cultural knowledge is defined as being a *"pool"* of information carried in the minds of individuals [JON 11]. It is established in the literature that the measure in which this information is shared varies. Thus, consensus analysis is not only interested in the content of an individual's mental models, but also in just how much there is an overlap of content or a shared understanding within a group of individuals.

Once again, the concepts are first identified by open discussions or open lists involving asking interviewees to list the relevant items, in their opinion, for a given subject. Second, a different group of interviewees will sort, classify and respond to questions to determine the similarity of the responses. Consensus analysis is a statistical analysis measuring the degree of consensus or, according to Jones *et al.* [JON 11] "shared knowledge" among individuals.

Broadly speaking, making mental models explicit does not stop at concepts that are considered important, but also studies the way in which they are organized from a cognitive point of view as well as their interactions. It involves understanding how people understand a system, how they believe that the system will respond to their interventions.

The similarities and differences in comprehension can be compared over time and space in order to increase the commensurability of the interpretative frameworks; in other words, to improve the overall understanding of a system by the individuals who are its components, making it possible to be aware of and understand an often-neglected kind of threat: the *insider threat.*

PART 2

The Insider Threat

3

The Three Categories of Insider Threats

Chapter 1 showed how artifacts have supported information systems through the ages and how human beings must understand these artifacts, whether they involve smoke signals, telegraphs or computer systems, to ensure the security of the information system. Chapter 2 presents the conclusion that while communication is natural for human beings, exchanging information in an information system supported by artifacts requires that the user be made aware of existing threats regarding the security of such an information system.

The massive computerization of information systems that occurred starting in the second half of the 20th Century has made it possible to reduce transmission and processing times and increase the quantities of information processed, but security flaws related to this computerization of information systems are perpetually discovered, tested and rediscovered. Computing is ubiquitous, leading to an omnipresence of access to information [NOJ 05, FRI 11]. Computing is resilient, safe and secured through procedures, fragments of code and infrastructures with known, controlled and rational behavior [PFL 02]. The result is that attacking a business' information system by targeting its digital component now is more of an intellectual and technological exercise than a utilitarian crime. In other words, the threat is no longer so much outside of organizations, whose firewalls are effective, and it no longer targets computers and digital artifacts, which have become more secure.

The threat is human and it is internal.

In this chapter, we will offer and explain a categorization of the insider threats with which an organization will be confronted. The reader will note that the future tense has been used here, but it could just as easily have been the past tense: between 2014 and 2015 the number of security incidents reported by organizations increased by 152% [PWC 16]. Indeed, an organization that has experienced an attack may not necessarily be conscious of it and, even when it is, it will not necessarily report it. The categorization of insider threats proposed in this book relies on two dimensions: (1) whether the character of the threat is intentional or not and (2) whether its character is malicious or not. These two dimensions are exposed and explained in this chapter, while the following part of the book focuses on the different insider threats that arise from this categorization.

At the beginning of the 1990s, the literature on information system security had already affirmed that there was "a gap between the use of modern technology and the understanding of the security implications inherent in its use" [LOC 92, p. 173]. The massive arrival of microcomputers was also accompanied by questions regarding the security of interconnected systems where computer science was previously mainframe-oriented, that is to say meant for a central computer. Indeed, the number of technological artifacts has exploded and this increase has gone hand in hand with the evolution of their various uses [CAN 15]. Yesterday, a terminal connected the user to the computer, while today entry points into the information system are multiple, universal, interconnected and increasingly discreet. Employees' social activity can be supported by social networks and their health maintained using connected watches.

The reader will note the disturbing current topicality of the taxonomy of threats targeting the security of information systems proposed by Loch *et al.* [LOC 92] presented in Figure 3.1, with regard to the four dimensions that make up his angle of analysis: (1) sources, (2) authors, (3) intentions and (4) consequences. It should be recognized that independent of the sources, authors and intentions of an attack, the consequences remain the same: disclosure (of profitable information), modification or destruction (of crucial information), or denial of service (by hindering access to resources). These consequences are covered in the 2013 ISO/IEC 27001 standard: information security management, which defines information security management systems as ensuring the (1) confidentiality, (2) integrity and (3) availability of information [ISO 13].

A business' firewall constitutes a protection against external threats, which appear on the left branch in Figure 3.1. Authors such as Willison and Warkentin [WIL 13] represent a part of the literature on information system security that tends to pay attention to insider threats, more particularly those whose authors are humans with the intention to cause harm (upper right branch in Figure 3.1).

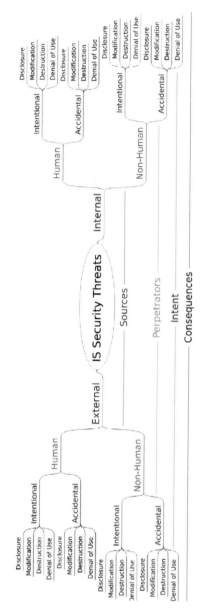

Figure 3.1. *Taxonomy of threats aimed at the security of information systems (from [LOC 92])*

The perspective provided by the previous section leads to reflection on the phenomena preceding an attack that come from the inside of the business, i.e. insider threats. Cognitive processes as well as organizational environments actually have an influence on the violation of an information system's security policy by an employee. From the point of view of this employee, who constitutes the entry point into the system, the violation of an information system's security policy can be:

1) *unintentional* (sector 1 in Figure 3.2): wrong actions taken by an inexperience or negligent employee, or one manipulated by an attacker; for example, an input error, accidental deletion of sensitive data, etc. [STA 05];

2) *intentional and non-malicious* (sector 2 in Figure 3.2): deliberate actions by an employee who derives a benefit but has no desire to cause harm; for example, deferring backups, choosing a weak password, leaving the door open during a sensitive discussion, etc. [GUO 11];

3) *intentional and malicious* (sector 3 in Figure 3.2): deliberate actions by an employee with a desire to cause harm [SHR 09]; for example, divulging sensitive data, introducing malicious software into the computer system, etc.

This latter category implies that the employee not only has privileged access, but also intimate knowledge of the internal organizational processes that allows him or her to exploit its weaknesses. Each one of these categories of violations of an information system's security policy is a category of *insider threat*. The rest of the book concentrates on these categories of insider threats.

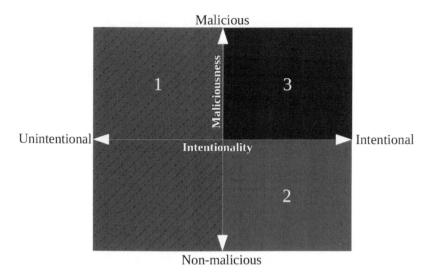

Figure 3.2. *Two dimensions and three categories of insider threats*

Thus, Chapter 4 focuses on the manipulation and social engineering techniques that exploit unintentional insider threats (category 1 above). Even though the attacker is outside of the system and the organization, he makes an employee, a component of the system, unintentionally facilitate its infiltration: the latter has, for example, clicked on a link or even opened the door to a self-proclaimed delivery person with a self-proclaimed task. This chapter exposes attack scenarios originating from unintentional insider threats.

Chapter 5 addresses situations where the employee has an interest in working around the information system's security policy to make every day work easier but has no desire to cause harm, creating intentional and non-malicious insider threats (category 2 above). These threats sometimes have no illegal character because of the absence of intention to cause harm, which makes them extremely difficult to thwart. Chapter 5 discusses a conceptual framework making it possible to understand workaround mechanisms and the intentional and non-malicious insider threats that they are likely to generate.

Finally, Chapter 6 concerns the organizational context and cognitive processes capable of leading employees toward becoming intentional and malicious insider threats (category 3 above). These employees then have the desire to cause harm and it can be possible – or not – to dissuade them. Indeed, this chapter also highlights the limits of dissuasion techniques used in organizations supported by the criminology literature and an analysis of the effectiveness of counter-measures with regard to specific context is proposed.

4

Unintentional

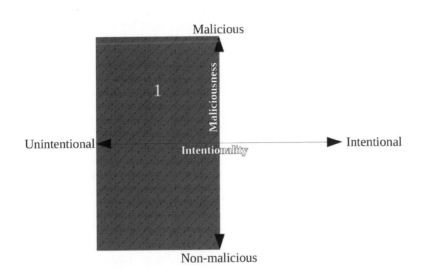

"Error, inattention and the lack of training and awareness constitute an unintentional insider threat to the information system's security. They can allow outside attackers to get through a business' firewall by targeting and manipulating legitimate users".

At the very beginning of the 2000s, cybersecurity expert B. Schneier, who had just created his business Counterpane

Internet Security Inc., posited that "security is a process, not a product" [SCH 00]. Security is not a matter of technology and artifacts; it is a matter of people and processes. The latter must be audited continually since, as new technological solutions are developed, the exploitation of hardware or software weaknesses will be more and more difficult. Attackers will then turn toward another component of the system susceptible to attack: the human one.

In [MIT 03, p. 14], breaching the human firewall is "easy", requiring no investment, except for occasional telephone calls, and minimum risk. The social engineer is very often friendly, and so charming and obliging that the target is happy to have met him.

The social engineer is an attacker who targets a legitimate user from whom he obtains a direct (rights of access, harmful link visited, etc.) or indirect (vital information, relationship of trust, etc.) means to get into the system.

Every legitimate user thus constitutes an unintentional insider threat to the information system's security, something which must be kept in mind when reinforcing and adapting the information system's security policy.

We are not trained to be suspicious of others. Additionally, we ourselves constitute the strongest threat to the security of the information system insofar as any well-prepared individual can win our trust. Computer experts have in fact developed more and more elaborate security solutions to reduce the risks related to the use of computers, but the greatest vulnerability remains the human factor. Indeed, remember that in the 1970s, the ARPANET (Advanced Research Projects Agency Network), which later would become the Internet, was created to allow major American universities and government institutions to share information. Very often these establishments installed little or no security in the first computer systems. Indeed, the goal was above all exchange that was as open as possible. Mitnick and Simon [MIT 03] even cite cases of "libertarians" opposed to protecting their accounts with a password. For them: "the dangers linked to a low level of security in our connected world have considerably evolved. And it is not by using more technologies that we till resolve the security problem related to the human factor" (p. 19). Starting in 2003 they have been drawing a parallel between the security of information systems and security in an airport. They then reflect on the flaw allowing travelers to take weapons on board while airports are in such a state of alert and are equipped with security devices such as metal detectors. The main security team must above all be trained to correctly sort the passengers, whatever the technological devices used. For the security of information systems, it is necessary to be informed about the techniques likely to be used to attack the confidentiality, integrity and availability of information [ISO 13], techniques that frequently target an entry point to which we are especially close: the human component of the information system.

In this chapter, some examples of attacks using social engineering techniques will be presented. The reader will see that these techniques can use digital means such as e-mails as shown in Figure 4.1, but they can also avoid them by concentrating on the individual independently of the tools with which he or she works. Figure 4.1 clearly shows the distinction between *phishing* and *spear phishing:* the second integrates social engineering techniques in order to win the target's trust and persuade him/her of the truthfulness of the information he/she receives.

This is to inform you that you have exceeded your email quota limit of 325MB and you need to increase your email quota limit because in less than 48 hours your email will be disable. Increase your email quota limit and continue to use your email account.

To increase your email quota limit to 2.2GB, , you must reply to (account-demo@gmx.com) this email immediately and enter your account details below.

Username: (**************)
Password: (**************)
Date Of Birth(************)

Failure to do this will immediately render your account deactivated from our database.

Thank you for your understanding.
Copyright © 2011 Webmail Helpdesk Support Centre.

a)

PayPal

This is an automated email, please do not reply

Information about your account :

Warning! Your PayPal account was limited!

Your account has been limited temporarily in order to protect it. The account will continue to be limited until it is approved.
Once you have updated your account records, your information will be confirmed and your account will start to work as normal once again.
The process does not take more than 5 minutes.
Once connected, follow the steps to activate your account. We appreciate your understanding as we work to ensure security.

Click here to Confirm Your Account Information.

Department review PayPal accounts

copyright 1999-2016 PayPal.All rights reserved
PayPal FSA Register Number:1388561750

PayPal Email ID PP156930

b)

Figure 4.1. *a) Phishing and b) spear phishing: the insider threat can be unintentional in the absence of awareness. For a color version of the figure, see www.iste.co.uk/arduin/insider.zip*

Indeed, note how the e-mail presented in Figure 4.1(a) is generic and impersonal. If there are elements implying urgency, for example "Failure to do this will immediately render your account deactivated from our database" (note the clumsy wording), they are crude in comparison to the injunctions of the e-mail presented in Figure 4.1(b): "Warning! Your PayPal account was limited!" Moreover, the second e-mail contains elements of color and visuals that are reassuring for the recipient, unlike in the first. The reader will doubtless think that these examples are obvious, but we wager that he or she would be surprised by the simplicity and the number of successful attacks that are due to the unintentional insider threat.

4.1. The quality of the stolen information

While an amateur attacker, also known as a "script kiddie", will be attracted by the quantity of the information available to steal, a professional attacker, such as a social engineer for example, will prefer the quality of the stolen information. Here, it is a question of the quality of the information in terms of the credibility that it brings to those who have it. Knowing the Wi-Fi password can allow you to access the network, certainly, but knowing the social security number of a senior executive or a director can allow you to do even more. A balance must nevertheless be found between security and productivity. When he receives an e-mail, a telephone call or reads these words, the reader needs to understand that he can, just like friends and colleagues, be manipulated. The reader should also be familiar with a sample of the manipulation techniques likely to be used.

The majority of protective tools sold on the market and deployed in large businesses mostly protects against script kiddies. The security of the business' information system goes through many mechanisms allowing (1) authentication for proving identity, (2) access control to manage access to resources and (3) the detection of intrusions to report suspect behavior. Nevertheless, the threat can come from inside of the business if employees are not made aware of social engineering techniques. An employee can authenticate themselves and access resources without an intrusion being detected insofar as he is a legitimate user, something which an external attacker can exploit through social engineering techniques. The legitimate user therefore becomes a potential unintentional insider threat.

Imagining that a computer is secure if it is turned off is unwise: a social engineer can simply persuade someone to turn it on.

This chapter will demonstrate attack scenarios that have been effective and illustrate the different facets of unintentional insider threats, especially the way in which they allow attackers to work around mechanisms allowing (1) authentication, (2) access control and (3) the detection of intrusions: they target legitimate users.

4.2. The case of apparently insignificant information that has hidden value

A malicious individual can harm a business' security simply by procuring certain information or documents, generally information that appears so trivial that the majority of employees do not see any reason not to reveal it. This apparently insignificant information is very useful to the social engineer for appearing credible. An employee may consider it insignificant when it is in fact not.

When an individual on the telephone knows the business' procedures, its jargon and insider information, it still does not identify him and neither does it authorize the individual to ask for information. Indeed, asking for something innocuous can lower the guard of a victim who would normally, if suspicious, ask for a name and a telephone number for example. Seeming friendly and using a little of the profession's jargon, or even joking, can encourage the other person to *trust*. The majority of people are short on time and verification requires time, which must be taken if an attack is supposed to be in progress.

Nevertheless, mastery of the internal vocabulary can make the social engineer appear authorized, with the victims becoming complacent despite themselves. A simple employee number, used in the right way, is equivalent to a password that the social engineer can use.

In addition, slipping in important questions among the other questions, which serve to provide credibility, makes it possible to avoid burning the source. "Burning the source" is when the victim becomes aware of the attack. He/she will then very probably warn colleagues and management, making it difficult to exploit this same source during later attacks.

Before asking a really important question, the social engineer might ask a test question, somewhat personal, and observe if the victim responds to it without his/her voice changing. This then means that she/he is not suspicious and that the important question can be asked without arousing suspicion.

After obtaining the key information, the social engineer will not end the conversation immediately but will instead add two or three other questions as well as some light conversation. The victim will remember the last moments of the exchanges, i.e. the lightness of the conversation along with the last two or three questions.

Here is an example of telephone exchanges where a social engineer obtains an employee number. It apparently involves unimportant information since it appears on practically all of the personal information forms that the employees fill out. Human resources, payroll and the external travel agency moreover have access to it.

- Hello Mr. Rocheleau, this is the Clap-Voyages travel agency. Your tickets for San Francisco are ready. Would you like us to send them to you or would you like to come get them yourself?	
- San Francisco? But I'm not traveling to San Francisco.	
- You are Daniel Rocheleau aren't you?	*[test question]* *Here the social engineer is testing whether the victim is suspicious or not.*
- Yes, but I'm not planning any trips in the near future.	
- Well… Are you sure that you don't want to go to San Francisco?	*[light question]* *Here the social engineer is seeking to gain the victim's sympathy.*
- If you think you can convince my boss…!	
-Well, it seems to me this was all just a misunderstanding. In our system, we record travel plans under the employee number. Maybe someone used the wrong one. What is your employee number?	*[important question]* *The social engineer, after having tested the victim and gained his sympathy, asks him for an apparently trivial piece of information.*

Scenario 4.1. *What is your employee number?*

The conversation continues in a light and friendly manner, but Daniel Rocheleau will have provided his employee number. Indeed, there is nothing confidential about this information. However, together with his name and, for example, his telephone number, it can make it possible to steal his identity.

In the following example, an apparently harmless e-mail is received by an employee who responds to it.

[test question]

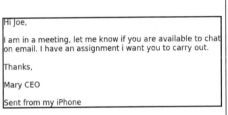

Hi Joe,

I am in a meeting, let me know if you are available to chat on email. I have an assignment i want you to carry out.

Thanks,

Mary CEO

Sent from my iPhone

Figure 4.2. *A seemingly harmless e-mail*

On the surface, there is nothing dangerous in this e-mail.

In reality, here the social engineer is testing whether or not the victim is suspicious. A response from someone who has not noticed the oddness of the signature ("Mary CEO") means that an unintentional insider threat exists.

Scenario 4.2. *Are you there?*

After having responded, the victim receives a second e-mail, which asks for his or her employee number in order to update a database of employees. Here again, this information is not confidential but, combined with his/her name and telephone number, it can make it possible to steal his/her identity.

In your organization, if a person claiming to be from another service contacted an employee and asked him/her for his employee number for a plausible reason, would he/she provide it?

4.3. The case of information that can simply be asked for

Sometimes a malicious person is able to obtain sensitive information from a business without having to get past security but simply by asking for them. Examples of this kind of attack, which are successful, are presented in this section.

The examples that follow (Scenarios 4.3 and 4.4) illustrate how an experienced social engineer can reach his or her goal because of a simple direct attack: when a demand appears reasonable, nothing seems to justify not satisfying it. The example given in Scenario 4.3 takes place late one evening, when the main office of a small telephone company receives a call. The operator responds and at the other end of the line is someone claiming to be from the business' reprography department.

- Good evening, this is reprography, we have your new list of test numbers, but for security reasons we cannot send them to you until we have received the old ones.	*[problem posed]* *The social engineer provides his/her interlocutor with a context and confronts them with a problem.*
- Test numbers? Ah...	
- The guy who delivers them is late, if you could just leave the old list at your door, he can make a detour, pick it up and leave the new one before continuing his route and that takes care of that.	*[solution proposed] [direct request]* *The social engineer makes a direct request to his interlocutor which solves the problem just posed.*
- No problem!	

Scenario 4.3. *Set it on the doorstep, thank you*

The list of test numbers provides information that is exploitable by any pirate, especially telephone numbers, allowing them to receive calls without them being traced back. The self-proclaimed reprography employee makes a direct request to the operator at the main office, who does exactly as instructed. He puts the copy on the doorstep of the building in an envelope indicating in big red letters: "BUSINESS CONFIDENTIAL – TO BE DESTROYED". All the attacker now has to do is come in a car, examine the surroundings, casually take the list and leave.

Scenario 4.4 indirectly implies the involvement of the vice-president of a large insurance company. It involves a special privilege frequently used in social engineering and constitutes a major unintentional insider threat in the sense that it has strong destructive potential.

- Hello, good evening this is Jerome from billing. I have a woman on the line here, a secretary of one of the company's vice-presidents, asking me for some information but I can't use my computer. I got an e-mail with the subject "I love you" from one of the girls in HR and since I opened the attachment I can't use my computer, it has a bad virus. Could you find some information for me?	*[direct request]* *The social engineer makes a direct request to his interlocutor who solves the problem which he has just been shown. He is relying on the position of "one of the vice-presidents" to establish his direct request.*
- Of course! That's terrible about the virus.	
- Yeah	
- What are you looking for?	
- Can you find an account in the customer billing information system?	

- No problem, what is the account number?	
- I don't have it! Maybe with the name...?	
- Yes, what is the name?	
- Morgana Tougas, t.o.u.g.a.s.	
- Okay, I have it.	
- Perfect, is it a current account?	
- Yes.	
- What is its number?	
- BAZ6573NR27Q	

Scenario 4.4. *It's for the vice-president*

After which Jerome rereads the number, he thanks the interlocutor and hangs up. It is interesting to see how in this attack the "I have someone on the line from the vice-president's office" technique is susceptible to work, just like the "This is Mr. Smith, from Management" one. It should not be assumed that social engineering attacks are very elaborate; rather they consist of going in, asking, taking and leaving, as in the examples presented above.

In your organization, if a person claiming to be acting on behalf of a well-known figure, of a director or a President, made an apparently reasonable request, would it be satisfied?

4.4. The case of the information that will help you

The attacker can spread information presenting him or herself as the person who can resolve a problem, which in reality does not exist. Figure 4.3 shows this technique, known as *reverse social engineering*: a web page that looks like a Microsoft Windows error page and encourages the user to call a telephone number to correct the self-proclaimed problem. In this case, it is the victim who contacts the attacker hoping that he will help resolve the self-proclaimed problem. A relationship of trust is projected by the victim toward the attacker who is now invested with the role of potential savior.

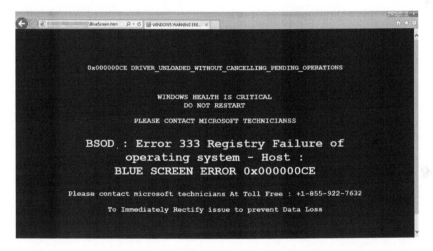

Figure 4.3. *A web page simulating a Microsoft Windows error screen*

In your organization, if an error seemed to have taken place and if a telephone number was displayed on the screen, would someone call it?

The victim will unintentionally become an entry point to be exploited by the attacker, who is still outside of the system. Training and raising awareness appear to be solutions that can lead to an understanding of the problem among employees. But these approaches demonstrate their limits when the insider threat is intentional and non-malicious, something that will be discussed in Chapter 5.

5

Intentional and Non-Malicious

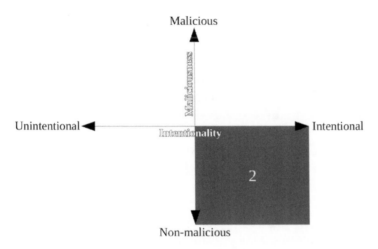

"The increasing complexity of a business' processes can lead employees to engage in workarounds meant to simplify their daily lives by modifying or ignoring the official procedures that exist. These workarounds constitute an intentional and non-malicious insider threat to the security of the information system insofar as the employees do not have the intention to cause harm"

As soon as several individuals are involved in carrying out an organization's activity, adjustment mechanisms must be set up to ensure the unity of the overall goal despite a division of labor. As a result, working alone to accomplish a goal is sometimes simpler than organizing the work of several people working toward the same goal.

Organizational structures are aimed at leading a group of people to belong to an "organized group". Recall that in the 12th Century, the Latin *organum* and the Greek ὄργανον (*órganon*) referred to a musical instrument or an organ of the body. In the 17th Century, "organized" was that which is arranged like an organ ([CNR 17], definition of organize). In French, the revolution and the end of the 18th Century would clarify the definition of an "organization" as the constitution of an institution, a public or private establishment ([CNR 17], definition of organization).

This organization establishes a certain number of rules ensuring the coherence of processes and it is these rules that are likely to make employees' daily tasks harder. They are sometimes seen as so many extra constraints that slow down work, and employees can be tempted to create "workarounds" by breaking these rules. Workarounds can admittedly be regarded as an unfavorable phenomenon, but also as a favorable phenomenon that should be taken advantage of. While the group unfavorable to workarounds considers them to be violations, which are resistant to intentions, expectations and the business' procedures [RÖD 14], the group favoring workarounds claims that they can be essential sources of information that must be analyzed to learn from policies, procedures and problems [ALT 14].

In this chapter, we will show the way in which we believe that certain workarounds can generate intentional and non-malicious insider threats to the security of information systems. Such threats can be regarded as an unfavorable phenomenon insofar as they violate the security policy of the business' information systems. Nevertheless, we posit that, with workarounds being inevitable, organizations must use them to identify new threats targeting the security of information systems and set up security policies adapted to their context.

5.1. Conflict between productivity and security

Workarounds represent the deliberate actions of employees who resist the instructions for the organization's functioning because these instructions make their daily tasks more difficult [ARD 17b]. Most of the time, these actions are perceived as being undesirable, especially because they lead to violations of the information systems' security policies.

Information system security is not just something that involves technology. It must be incorporated into a technology implementation strategy carried out consistently and closer to the ground. A robust infrastructure certainly makes it possible to provide a technological environment within which a form of security is attainable, yet when the digital information system goes into production, its appropriation by users leads to possible changes, some profitable and others dangerous for the system's security. These changes cannot have been taken into consideration from the beginning. Indeed, while employees have an increasing desire for technology, threats, particularly those coming from the inside, continue to increase [RÖD 14, SIL 14].

Information system security must take into account the relationships between individuals, processes and technologies [SIL 14]. If a conflict arises between productivity in daily tasks and the security of the information system, resistance will emerge on the part of the users [PFL 02]. In this case, users will take advantage of the system's flexibility to short-circuit its functions and engage in workarounds [PAV 10].

The security policies of information systems are too often constructed without sufficiently taking into account their impact on employees' productivity in their daily tasks.

This kind of negligence encourages workarounds. In [ALT 14], workarounds are situations in which individuals will intentionally perform actions running counter to one or several routines, standards or official instructions in order to get around technical or organizational constraint. The literature agrees on the fact that workarounds are inevitable within organizations [SUC 07, GYÖ 12]. In recent years, the literature has also focused on the identification of factors, which lead to workarounds or which make it possible to predict the intention of certain employees to engage in workarounds [CHU 14, JOH 13].

As shown in Figure 5.1, it is the adjustment between constraints on the ground (*bottom-up*) and strategic pressure (*top-down*), which explains the occurrence and persistence of workarounds [AZA 12]. A side effect of workarounds is that they represent an intentional and non-malicious insider threat for the security of the organization's information system: ignoring password modification procedures, post-poning backups, leaving a door open during a sensitive conversation, etc. Sometimes managers will tacitly approve workarounds if the activity's continuity is not challenged [RÖD 14].

In Figure 5.1, the adjustment that must be made between constraints on the ground and strategic pressures is represented by the arrows pointing in opposite directions. This adjustment leads to workarounds implemented by employees to bypass a form of security considered too restrictive (horizontal line) to achieve productivity in their daily tasks (diagonal line). This fragile balance is also shown in Figure 5.3.

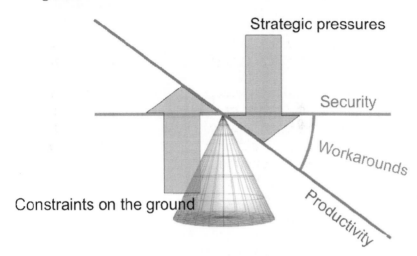

Figure 5.1. *Workarounds: an adjustment between constraints on the ground (bottom-up) and strategic pressures (top-down)*

In this way, the balance that needs to be found between productivity and the security of tasks can cause dilemmas for employees in which they must choose between productivity and security. Workarounds can be seen as creative actions and sources of future improvements [ARD 17b], as well as pure and simple violations of information systems' security policies [PFL 02]. The consequence can thus involve innovation or risk, as shown in Figure 5.2.

Figure 5.2. *A caricatural workaround showing the innovation and risk aspects*

5.2. Workarounds, a factor for innovation or risk

Defining a security policy for an information system is a crucial task that requires being conscious of user behaviors within the organization [SIL 14]. Indeed, intentional and non-malicious insider threats are explained as much as they are justified because the user has the intention to bypass a technical or organizational constraint using a workaround, without desire to cause harm.

In [JOH 13], security that puts too much of a burden on employees and is not aligned with their practices becomes less and less effective. The excess can be direct (multiplication of authentication procedures for example) or indirect (moving too far away from official procedures with the procedures currently in place for example). The employees can then reasonably estimate that the cost of respect for procedures is greater than the security benefit obtained. As a result, they engage in workarounds.

Beautement *et al.* [BEA 16] emphasize the fact that almost no organization evaluates whether or not its information system's security policies are adapted to the reality of the work environment, that is, if the information system's security policy does not encourage employees to implement workarounds. Concepts such as "information security awareness" are supposed to change employees' work habits and lead them to secure information processing practices [TSO 15]. Indeed, a centralized vision of security shows its limits and managers must rethink the way in which the security of information systems is conceived, implemented and managed [SIL 14].

5.2.1. *Workarounds are an innovation*

Workarounds are implemented by employees not through deliberate neglect of security policies but rather by necessity in order to effectively carry out their daily tasks. Knowledge of the field, experience and practices leading certain employees to create new knowledge of the field, new experiences and new practices, which make the information system's security policy more adapted to their organization and their daily tasks. In this sense, workarounds can be seen as innovation factors within the organization.

5.2.2. *Workarounds are a risk*

Non-malicious violations of the information system's security policy are defined as being "the behaviors engaged in by end users who knowingly violate organizational IS security policies without malicious intents to cause damage" [GUO 11, p. 205]. Workarounds can thus lead to non-malicious violations of the information system's security policy, which have this characteristic to constitute a non-malicious insider threat, admittedly, but also an intentional one. By violating the information system's security policy through a workaround, an employee exposes its activity to attacks. Within this context, workarounds can be seen as risk factors in the organization.

5.3. On non-malicious violations

In [GUO 11], non-malicious violations of the security policy of an organization's information system have four characteristics: (1) intentional behaviors, (2) personal benefit without malicious intent, (3) voluntary breaking of the rules and (4) possible damage or risk to security. These characteristics highlight the way in which a workaround, constituting an intentional and non-malicious insider threat, can simultaneously threaten the information system's security and provide instructions making it possible to ensure its security (see Figure 5.3). Furthermore, the instructions for the information system's security policy, if they ensure the information system's security, can also lead to workarounds (see Figure 5.3).

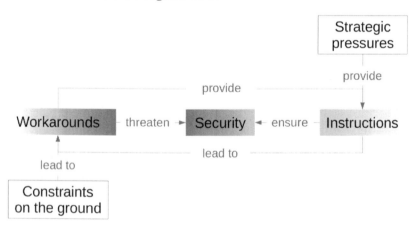

Figure 5.3. *The fragile balance of security when the threat is internal, intentional and non-malicious: workarounds*

The first two non-malicious violations of an information system's security policy (intentional behaviors and personal benefit without malicious intent) emphasize this special characteristic of the workarounds: they correspond to intentional, non-malicious and ethical behaviors. The two latter characteristics (voluntary breaking of the rules and possible damage or risk to security) emphasize this other characteristic of workarounds: instructions were violated and the perceived security risk was low. New knowledge generated by this violation, namely how employees can work around the information system's security policy, must be valued insofar as they provide new instructions for the development of an information system's security policy better in line with the context of the organization.

5.3.1. Intentional behavior

Workarounds are intentional and the employees are making decisions reasonably when they intentionally engage in workarounds. This characteristic removes all unintentional threats such as those addressed in Chapter 4: the lack of awareness, errors and social engineering. On its own, this characteristic does not make the distinction between the malicious, such as sharing sensitive data, and the non-malicious, such as postponing a backup.

5.3.2. Personal benefit without malicious intent

These are organizational or technical constraints that generate workarounds. Employees are looking for a personal benefit in their daily tasks. In [GUO 11], the employees who engage in non-malicious violations of the information system's security policy (1) have no malicious intent, such as harming the security or activities of the organization, and (2) are not carrying out immoral actions at the expense of the organization for their personal benefit, such as stealing and selling sensitive information. In other words, this characteristic highlights the fact that workarounds are difficult to subject to legal proceedings.

Intentional and non-malicious insider threats are difficult to subject to legal proceedings insofar as there is no intention to cause harm.

5.3.3. *Voluntary breaking of the rules*

By imagining, creating and engaging in workarounds, employees are violating instructions and the standards established for business processes. Even if these instructions and these standards are compulsory, employees can violate them intentionally for their personal benefit without malicious intent, as expressed in the two previous characteristics. This voluntary breaking of the rules is likely to threaten the security of the information system, all the while disclosing behaviors and uses that it is important to consider in establishing a security policy for the information system that best fits the organization's constraints.

5.3.4. *Possible damage or risk to security*

As violations of instructions and the standards established for operational procedures, workarounds are likely to generate damage or security risks. If employees perceive low security risks they are likely to more easily engage in workarounds, which will therefore be more difficult to deter [DAR 12]. The perception of security risk is thus a potential catalyst, one which must be taken into account when establishing the information system's security policy. The question is knowing where to place the cursor between "feel free to innovate" and "scrupulously carry out the procedure" in order to allow the organization's activity to be carried out effectively and in complete security.

Deterrence approaches will, nevertheless, show their limits when the insider threat is intentional and malicious, which will be addressed in Chapter 6.

6

Intentional and Malicious

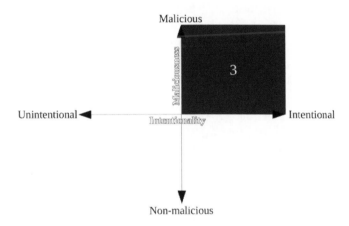

"One of the greatest fears of a chief information officer is the employee who has privileged access, who has intimate knowledge of the organization's processes and who becomes an intentional and malicious insider threat. This insider threat is not only difficult to detect, it is difficult to deter if we do not seek to understand the organizational and cognitive factors which contribute to committing the act".

Unlike the unintentional or intentional and non-malicious insider threats discussed in Chapters 4 and 5, respectively, intentional and malicious insider threats have this characteristic of *intention to cause harm* on the part of an employee located within the organization. Every employee is in fact a component of the information system likely to constitute a threat. If cases of unintentional (Chapter 4) or intentional and non-malicious (Chapter 5) threats are to be monitored, cases of intentional and malicious threats require special attention: understanding them to better anticipate them.

We will start this chapter with the true story of an intentional and malicious insider threat, which led a bank to lose several millions of dollars in the context of 1970s computing, still centralized and reserved for technology experts. The reader will see how attack procedures used by an employee who constitutes an intentional and malicious insider threat can be exactly the same many years later. We will then propose to focus on organizational and cognitive factors likely to lead an employee to become an intentional and malicious insider threat, in other words the factors involved in "committing the act". Finally, we will see which analyses to conduct in order to use desirable – if not urgent – deterrent mechanisms that are above all effective, depending on the specific context.

6.1. The information is known; why not exploit it?

In 1978, Stanley Rifkin was a consultant at Security Pacific National Bank (Figure 6.1), where he worked on the development of a system meant to back up the transfer room's data, in cases where the principal computer failed. He has strong knowledge of the transfer procedures and especially of the way in which the bank's employees worked to make a transfer: each morning, they were given a closely guarded code that they used to call the transfer room and order wire transfers. Most of the time, the employees wrote this code on a code Post-it note each morning, which they put in a place where they could read it easily.

On a November morning, Rifkin made a visit to the transfer room, whence wires totaling billions of dollars were sent and received every day, allegedly to take some notes on the operating procedures and ensure that the backup system he was responsible for was well coordinated with traditional systems. In reality, Rifkin was above all interested in the Post-its. He discreetly read an employee's security code, learned it by heart and left a few minutes later. At that moment, as he would later say, he felt like he had won the lottery.

Figure 6.1. *The Security Pacific National Bank building in 1971 (source: Robert Clements and Associates)*

After leaving the transfer room, he went directly to a telephone booth located in the building's hall and called the transfer room pretending to be Mike Hansen, a member of the bank's international service. Here is how their telephone conversation would have gone.

- Hello, this is Mike Hansen from International.	
- Hello, Mike. What is your office number? - 286	*[control]* *This was standard procedure and this information was public and therefore Rifkin knew it.*
- OK; what is the security code? - 4789. You have to make a wire transfer of exactly ten million, two hundred thousand dollars to the Irving Trust Company in New York for the credit of the Wozchod Handelsbank in Zurich.	*[control]* *He then responds calmly with the code that he had learned by heart in the transfer room, then gives instructions for sending a wire to a Swiss bank where he already had an account.*
- Very good. Now I need the interoffice establishment number. - Let me verify it. I will call you back.	*[control]* *Rifkin begins to sweat; this question was not expected, but he was able to maintain his calm and continue speaking to his interlocutor without pausing.*

Scenario 6.1. *The Post-it in the transfer room*

He then called another of the bank's services, this time pretending to be an employee from the transfer room to obtain the number. He then called the woman back, and she took note and thanked him.

Several days later, Rifkin flew to Switzerland and bought eight million dollars worth of diamonds from a Russian company, which he brought back to the United States hidden in a money belt. Without a gun or a computer, he had carried out the largest bank robbery in history. A meticulous plan and smooth talk were all that was required. These are the skills and techniques that we group together under the term of social engineering.

In your organization, many years after Rifkin constituted an intentional and malicious insider threat to Security Pacific National Bank, how many employees have privileged access which they might decide to exploit? What means of deterrence and detection do you have access to? Have you determined their effectiveness?

6.2. Organizational environment and cognitive processes of committing the act

While the academic literature takes a timid interest in the question of what leads an "insider" to act, organizations concerned refrain from communicating about highly sensitive subjects: the employee who becomes an intentional and malicious insider threat, with his privileged access and his knowledge of the organization, becomes an attacker.

In section 6.2.1, we will explore deterrence in history and in the present. This countermeasure is indeed often used against intentional and malicious insider threats. In section 6.2.2, we will analyze elements of the criminology literature to confront them with information system security. In doing this, we will have addressed the organizational context as well as the cognitive processes that underlie committing the act: why (organizational context) and how (cognitive processes) does an employee become an attacker?

6.2.1. *For the organization, deterrence prevents maliciousness*

Straub and Welke [STR 98] have proposed an action cycle for managing the security of information systems by focusing more specifically on insider threats, whose authors are humans with the intention to cause harm. This cycle includes (1) deterrence, (2) prevention, (3) detection and (4) remedies. Thus, for these authors, the violation of an information system's security policy from the inside can be avoided by deterring dishonest employees from committing an attack, which is the first part of the action cycle. Setting up prevention measures, the second part of the action cycle, may prevent dishonest employees who have not been deterred from committing an attack. In practice, in an organization, posters constitute a deterrence measure and the blocking of peripheral devices constitute a prevention measure, for example. If an attack occurs in spite of everything, it must be detected, which is the goal of the third part of the action cycle. The last part consists of setting up remedies following successful attacks. In every case, the second, third and fourth parts of the action cycle can provide the new elements of deterrence (see Figure 6.2).

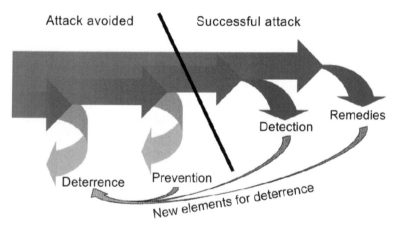

Figure 6.2. *Straub–Welke's security action cycle (from [STR 98])*

A line can be drawn here between the security of information systems and public health. Figure 6.3, for example, compares a deterrent public health poster in 1942 (a) and one for the security of information systems in 2003 (b). In [STR 98], displays in businesses have value as a deterrent. Even if it is only informative as presented in Figure 6.3, it can mention potential economic sanctions. Prevention is more intrusive insofar as it can involve, for example, the closing of USB ports or the control of telephone calls.

a) (Source: U.S. National Archives and Records Administration, 1942)

b) (Source: [WIL 03])

Figure 6.3. *a) A deterrent public health poster in 1942 and b) an information systems security deterrent poster in 2003*

Deterrence, nevertheless, demonstrates its limits when the attacker, an employee, justifies the attack by means of cognitive processes of moral disengagement, which has already been understood by the criminology literature and which we will now present.

6.2.2. *For the employee, moral disengagement justifies maliciousness*

We now focus all of our attention on the individual and on the cognitive processes that he or she is likely to set up to morally disengage and justify his or her committing the action. To do this, we will mobilize elements of the criminology literature and confront them with the security of information systems.

In criminology literature, the way in which an individual attempts to rationalize or justify his or her criminal behavior is analyzed. Authors such as Sykes and Matza [SYK 57] have, for example, shown that the internalization of norms, that is to say an individual's appropriation of social and societal standards, can have deterrent effect and an influence on the decision to engage in a criminal behavior. However, they call the mechanisms through which an individual can clear away internalized norms and social censure "neutralization techniques": "by a subtle alchemy, the delinquent moves himself into the position of an avenger and the victim is transformed into a wrong-doer" [SYK, p. 668]. Through these moral disengagement mechanisms, an individual can justify deviant or criminal behavior and thus move in this direction without feeling guilt or shame. Since these feelings have a deterrent effect similar to punishment, neutralization techniques can thus be used by an individual to reduce them. They thus find themselves free to commit the act. Here, we see some of the neutralization techniques studied in the criminology literature and relevant to information system security:

1) *Denial of illegality* [GEL 86]: "It's not illegal, so I have the right to do it". The individual excuses malicious practices due to the fact that they are not illegal.

2) *Denial of responsibility* [SYK 57]: "It's not my fault; I had no other choice". The individual relies on routine or authority to explain that he had no other choice than the one he made.

Circumstances outside of his control have constrained him: orders from management, pressure from colleagues, desperate financial situation, existence of precedents, etc.

3) *Denial of injury* [SYK 57]: "Nobody was hurt". The individual relies on the organization's capacity to reabsorb costs because it has insurance. He thinks that insofar as no one was actually hurt, his actions are not malicious. Horning [HOR 70] showed that close to one-third of employees of an assembly plant do not consider the theft of merchandise by their peers as theft.

4) *Denial of the victim* [SYK 57]: "They really deserved it". The individual refuses to grant victim status to the victim. For him or her, the victim could have deserved it because of past activities, or could have desired and caused his/her status.

5) *Condemnation of accusers* [SYK 57]: "Everyone is dishonest". The individual casts doubt on the legitimacy of those who accuse him in order to establish his own malicious actions.

6) *Appeal to higher loyalties* [SYK 57]: "I didn't do it for myself". The individual claims that universal ethical norms had to be sacrificed for greater causes, the most common being loyalty to a group. Groups indeed see their own interests as higher than those of other groups or society.

7) *Metaphor of the ledger* [KLO 74]: "I've done so many good things in my life, so just this once...". The individual thinks that it is possible to accumulate good points by performing good actions which he or she can then redeem to carry out bad ones.

Criminology literature states that shame has a deterrent effect similar to punishment. Neutralization techniques mentioned above are used by individuals to lessen feelings of shame or guilt when malicious or deviant actions are committed. Since these feelings have a deterrent effect, their absence can leave an employee free to act, with the result that:

The use of neutralization techniques by an employee can make it possible to predict his intention of violating the security policy of the business' information systems.

Indeed, in [SIP 10], "neutralization is an excellent predictor of employees' intention to violate IS security policies"(p.10). In addition, observing an employee within the business using neutralization techniques can constitute a red flag, indicating his or her intention to violate the information system security policy. It should be noted, however, that neutralization techniques are only relevant for those who are partially engaged in a malicious behavior. Employees fully engaged in a malicious behavior as well as those fully engaged in a non-malicious behavior feel no need to neutralize their behavior (see Figure 6.4).

Non-malicious

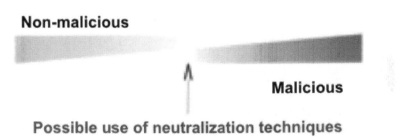

Malicious

Possible use of neutralization techniques

Figure 6.4. *Point between a fully malicious employee (right), fully non-malicious employee (left) and one likely to use neutralization techniques (center)*

6.3. Ease of deterrence

In [WIL 13], motivation can influence the measure in which it is possible to deter an intentional and malicious insider threat to the security of an information system. Criminology literature proposes classifying attacks according to two categories of motivations: instrumental motivations and expressive motivations. In the first case, the malicious actions are the means of achieving a goal. The attacker can, for example, commit an aggressive act to get money; aggression is thus the instrument used to obtain the money. In the second case, the attacker can feel frustration, anger or despair and the malicious actions are the purpose of the attack.

The instrumental/expressive motivations distinction has been used by criminologists to understand crimes such as terrorism, rape, vandalism, workplace violence, domestic violence, arson and violent street crime (see [WIL 13] for an extensive bibliography on these subjects). A specific crime cannot, nevertheless, be classified as instrumental or expressive. Homicide, for example, is a case where the border between instrumental motivations and expressive motivations is blurred.

The ease with which an intentional and malicious insider threat can be deterred is an essential question in ensuring the security of information systems. This ease of deterrence can be understood through a three-dimensional prism; an illustration is shown in Figure 6.5. This prism, introduced in [ARD 17a], was developed from elements in the criminology literature juxtaposed with real cases of insider threats targeting the security of information systems, which constitute the originality of the work presented in this book. The three dimensions of the prism are the following:

– *Motivation*: expressive attacks have their source in emotions. These bring the individual to what he/she feels in the present moment. The benefits are thus more obvious than the repercussions. The decision-making process (toward committing the act) takes place in a narrowed and distorted time, which explains why the individual is likely to behave in ways apparently contrary to his or her own interest. So, attacks with expressive motivations are more difficult to deter than those with instrumental motivations.

– *Speed*: an attacker who takes the time to decide before acting exposes themselves to repercussions that are likely to deter him or her (see section 6.2.2). Zimring and Hawkins [ZIM 73] have put forward the hypothesis that the more quickly an attacker decides to act, the less he is likely to be deterred. The attacker acting slowly actually retains a capacity for reflection, which will show him the consequences of the action. So, attacks carried out quickly are more difficult to deter than those carried out slowly.

– *Engagement*: the attacker's level of criminal engagement makes him more or less receptive to repercussions and – in fact – to deterrence. It corresponds to the measure in which the attacker is leading a "criminal way of life" [CHA 67]. So, attacks in which the attacker is very criminally engaged are more difficult to deter than those in which the attacker is not very criminally engaged.

Beyond this focus on the attacker, an employee who justifies an attack by means of cognitive processes, the organizational context must also be understood. Indeed, management can lead to grievances likely to set off the activation of said cognitive processes. Managerial innovation [ARD 17a] can be seen as a possible response allowing knowledge and management of the security of information systems from the point of view of technologies, certainly, but also the people who are employed by the business.

In fact, a study conducted by Keeney *et al.* [KEE 05] of a sample of 49 attacks committed by employees violating the information system security policy, reported that in 83% of cases, the employee attacker had a work-related grievance. This kind of grievance acts as a release mechanism. Factors of dissatisfaction actually have a significant impact on the information system's security insofar as an unhappy employee will more likely commit an attack by violating the security policy of his company's information systems. He or she will become an intentional and malicious insider threat.

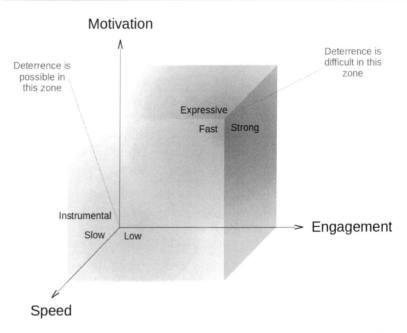

Figure 6.5. *Ease of deterring a violation of the information system security policy when the threat is internal, intentional and malicious*

Although the focus can be placed on the attack and its consequences, the immediate antecedents should not be neglected. Military jargon actually calls the elements observable before an incident "pre-kinetic events" [ALL 09]. Thus, the potential attacker's thought processes should be considered as well as how he or she has been influenced by the organizational context. The interaction between thought processes and organizational context can significantly impact the effectiveness of the deterrence, especially when studying (1) the attacker's motivations, (2) the speed of the attack and (3) the attacker's level of criminal engagement, as discussed in this chapter.

Factors that are located outside of the traditional field of information systems' security have strong implications in this field. While past research has called for concentration on digital artifacts, this chapter and this book open the way to productive exchanges about innovative management of individuals and machines, where the information system would see its security ensured through virtuous, robust and lasting relationships between all of its components: technologies and people.

Conclusion

Intelligence, as discussed in the foreword of this book, is the capacity that we have to link ideas with each other: *inter-ligare*. As for information, it links individuals who shape their knowledge: *in-forme-atio*. Intelligence and information thus converge toward this idea of linking, whether it is ideas or people. What if information systems were only the expression of a need which has animated human beings since the beginning of time? The need for exchange and interaction. We are communicating beings, trusting by default, sometimes distracted, inventive through carelessness and sometimes malicious. The threat can also come from the inside.

The explosion of technologies has paradoxically given individuals a larger and larger place in organizations' information systems. Entry points are everywhere, universal, ubiquitous, interoperating, interconnected and more and more subtle. Each one of us is susceptible to undergoing attacks through social engineering techniques aimed at deceiving us and making us let an attacker into the system in spite of ourselves. Is this deliveryman asking me to keep the door open really a deliveryman? Why is this assistant asking me to me send an e-mail to a colleague? Should I click on this link to update my password (which I haven't changed for 15 years)? In your organization, these questions are raised and must be raised. The threat which hangs over the information system's security must be considered, especially when it is internal since it is too often neglected.

In the first part of this book, Chapters 1 and 2 highlight the purposes of technologies and the specificities of individuals as components of the information system. While technologies first allowed a decrease in transmission times and then processing times, electronic computing has led organizations to confront the massification of quantities of information. Each technological upheaval has disclosed new weaknesses exploitable by attackers, driving disciplines such as cryptography and critical systems to make computer science safe and secured. The trend is thus reversed and individuals have (re)taken their place in the attackers' crosshairs. Each person is an interpretive component whose behavior is sometimes irrational, a processor that is easily manipulated through procedures known and tested by social engineers. Attacking an organization's information system by targeting its technological component is now more of an intellectual and technical exercise than a utilitarian crime. In other words, the threat is no longer outside of organizations, whose firewalls are effective, and no longer targets computers and digital artifacts, which have become too secure: the threat is human and it is internal.

From the first part of this book, the reader will remember from Chapter 1 that once it is supported by an artifact, an information system presents security weaknesses that we are not naturally aware of. Communication by voice leads us to take precautions from a very young age such as closing a door or paying attention to who might be listening to us, unlike communicating through an artifact, whether it is a computer, a Chappe telegraph or a network of torches; even more so when artifacts change, appear and become obsolete at a great speed. In Chapter 2, we discussed how not only knowledge results from the interpretation of information by an individual, but also that language, whether natural or scientific, can be interpreted differently. This plasticity of the human psyche makes us simultaneously a force for innovation and risk. We can fail to understand, trust, be distracted, work around the rules, or even be malicious. All of this constitutes *a priori* many insider threats to the information system's security.

In the second part of this book, Chapter 3 exposes a categorization of insider threats, which are presented in Chapters 4-6. Based on the academic literature, international standards, as well as on observations made in the field, this categorization is built around two dimensions: (1) whether the character of the insider threat is intentional or not and (2) its malicious character. Three categories of insider threat follow: (1) the unintentional, (2) the intentional and non-malicious and (3) the intentional and malicious. Chapter 4 focuses on unintentional insider threats, when a person facilitates infiltration by an attacker despite themselves. Through an excess of trust or from lack of awareness, this person can, for example, click on a link or let in a self-proclaimed deliveryman. If awareness and training are presented as responses, they, nevertheless, reach their limits when the insider threat becomes intentional and non-malicious: this is the focus of Chapter 5. Through inventiveness or through carelessness, the person thus has an interest in working around the information system security policy to make daily tasks easier, but without desire to cause harm. The absence of an illegal character, since there is no intention to cause harm, makes these threats difficult to thwart and if deterrence seems to be a response, it nevertheless reaches its limits when the insider threat becomes intentional and malicious, which is addressed in Chapter 6. The person thus has the intention to harm the organization and the focus is on the organizational context and cognitive processes, which have led this individual, employed by an organization, to become an intentional and malicious insider threat. It is thus possible – or not – to deter him/her from committing the act, which is discussed in this chapter.

From part two of this book, the reader will remember from Chapter 4 that the social engineer is an attacker who targets a legitimate user to obtain a direct (rights of access, harmful link visited, etc.) or indirect (vital information, relationship of trust, etc.) means to get into the system. Thus, imagining a computer safe if it is turned off is unwise: a social engineer can simply persuade someone to turn it on. Before asking a truly important question, the social engineer might ask a test question, somewhat personal, and observe if the victim responds to it without his/her voice changing. This then means that he/she is not suspicious and that the important question can be asked without arousing suspicion. The reader will remember from Chapter 5 that security policies of information systems are too often constructed without sufficiently taking into account their impact on the productivity of employees in their everyday tasks. This distance between security and productivity is likely to create workarounds leading to intentional and non-malicious insider threats, which are difficult to subject to legal proceedings insofar as there is no intention to cause harm. Finally, in Chapter 6 we discussed how the use of neutralization techniques by an employee may make it possible to predict his intention to violate the business' information system security policy.

This book opens with the question of knowing how to ensure the security of an information system by taking into account individuals as components whose behavior is sometimes irrational. It has shown that the exchange of information between people was supported by artifacts well before the introduction of computers. These artifacts have their purposes and their weaknesses that lead to so many threats, but other threats exist. The organization as an organized system has borders and threats can also be found inside of these borders. Individuals act as interpretive agents: they create their knowledge from information that they perceive through their interpretative frameworks. They share this knowledge by creating information through interpretative frameworks and this creation can differ from one person to another. They can trust, be distracted, inventive, careless and sometimes malicious. People are human and this humanity does not make them a threat strictly speaking. The real insider threat is to neglect the specificities of the individuals who make up the organization. Computing is only the automatic processing of information and we must pay attention to what else, central and non-automatizable, the individual can bring to the organization. The threat can be internal, certainly, but so are the unexpected, creativity, and hope.

Bibliography

[ABE 98] ABEL N., ROSS H., WALKER P., "Mental models in rangeland research, communication and management", *The Rangeland Journal*, vol. 20, pp. 77–91, 1998.

[ALL 09] ALLEN J., The Combat Operator, *DefenseTech*, March 23, 2009.

[ALT 14] ALTER S., "Theory of workarounds", *Communications of the Association for Information Systems*, vol. 34, pp. 1041–1066, 2014.

[ARD 13] ARDUIN P.-E., Vers une métrique de la commensurabilité des schémas d'interprétation, PhD Thesis, Paris-Dauphine University, 2013.

[ARD 15] ARDUIN P.-E., GRUNDSTEIN M., ROSENTHAL-SABROUX C., *Information and Knowledge System,* ISTE Ltd, London, and John Wiley & Sons, New York, 2015.

[ARD 17a] ARDUIN P.-E., "Sécurité des systèmes d'information: de la criminologie à l'innovation managériale", in PERRET V., NOGATCHEWSKY G. (eds), *L'état des entreprises 2017,* La Découverte, Paris, pp. 63–75, 2017.

[ARD 17b] ARDUIN P.-E., VIERU D., "Workarounds as Means to Identify Insider Threats to Information Systems Security", *Twenty-third Americas Conference on Information Systems*, Boston, August 10–12, 2017.

[AZA 12] AZAD B., KING N., "Institutionalized computer workaround practices in a Mediterranean country: an examination of two organizations", *European Journal of Information Systems*, vol. 21, no. 4, pp. 358–372, 2012.

[BEA 16] BEAUTEMENT A., BECKER I., PARKIN S. *et al.*, "Productive security: a scalable methodology for analyzing employee security behaviors", SOUPS, Denver, CO, 2016.

[BOU 06] BOUNFOUR A., EPINETTE G., *Valeur et performance des si: une nouvelle approche du capital immatériel de l'entreprise*, Dunod, Paris, 2006.

[BRY 08] BRYANT A., "The future of information systems – thinking informatically", *European Journal of Information Systems*, vol. 17, pp. 695–698, 2008.

[CAM 98] CAMINER D.T., ARIS J.B.B., HERMON P.M.R., *et al.*, *LEO: The Incredible Story of the World's First Business Computer*, McGraw-Hill, New York, 1998.

[CAN 15] CANOHOTO A.I., DIBB S., SIMKIN L. *et al.*, "Preparing for the future – how managers perceive, interpret and assess the impact of digital technologies for business", *Proceedings of the 48th Hawaii International Conference on System Sciences*, Kauai, HI, 2015.

[CAR 92] CARLEY K., PALMQUIST M., "Extracting, representing, and analyzing mental models", *Social Forces*, vol. 70, no. 3, pp. 601–636, 1992.

[CHA 67] CHAMBLISS W., "Types of deviance and the effectiveness of legal sanctions", *Wisconsin Law Review*, vol. 3, pp. 703–719, 1967.

[CHU 14] CHUA C., STOREY V., CHEN L., *Central IT or shadow IT? Factors shaping users' decision to go rogue with IT*, ICIS, Auckland, 2014.

[CNR 17] CNRTL, Centre National de Ressources Textuelles et Lexicales, available at: http://www.cnrtl.fr, 2017.

[COL 87] COLLINS A., GENTNER D., "How people construct mental models", in HOLLAND D., QUINN N. (eds), *Cultural Models in Language and Thought*, Cambridge University Press, Cambridge, 1987.

[CRA 43] CRAIK K.J.W., *The Nature of Explanation*, Cambridge University Press, Cambridge, 1943.

[DAN 95] D'ANDRADE R., *The Development of Cognitive Anthropology*, Cambridge University Press, Cambridge, 1995.

[DAN 01] DANIELS R.B., BEELER J., "An archival investigation of a late 19th century accounting information system: the use of decision aids in the american printing industry", *The Accounting Historians Journal*, vol. 28, no. 1, pp. 3–18, 2001.

[DAR 14] D'ARCY J., HERATH T., SHOSS M., "Understanding employee responses to stressful information security requirements: a coping perspective", *Journal of Management Information Systems*, vol. 31, no. 2, pp. 285–318, 2014.

[DAF 84] DAFT R.L., WEICK K.E., "Toward a model of organizations as interpretation systems", *The Academy of Management Review*, vol. 9, no. 2, pp. 284–295, 1984.

[DOW 76] DOWNS R.M., "Cognitive mapping and information processing: a commentary", in MOORE G.T., GOLLEDGE R.G. (eds), *Environmental knowing: theories, research, and methods*, Dowden, Hutchinson & Ross, Oxford, 1976.

[DRA 06] DRAY A., PEREZ P., JONES N. *et al.*, "The AtollGame experience: from knowledge engineering to a computer-assisted role playing game", *Journal of Artificial Societies and Social Simulation*, vol. 9, no. 1, pp. 1–11, 2006.

[DRA 07] DRAY A., PEREZ P., JONES N. *et al.*, "Who wants to terminate the game? The role of vested interests and metaplayers in the ATOLLGAME experience", *Simulation and Gaming*, vol. 38, pp. 494–511, 2007.

[ETI 11] ETIENNE M., DU TOIT D.R., POLLARD S., "ARDI: a co-construction method for participatory modeling in natural resources management", *Ecology and Society*, vol. 16, no. 1, p. 44, 2011.

[FIG 68] FIGUIER L., *Les Merveilles de la science ou description populaire des inventions modernes*, Furne, Jouvet and Cie, Paris, 1868.

[FON 05] FONTENELLE B., "Éloge de Guillaume Amontons par FONTENELLE", in BOUDOT J. (ed.), *Histoire de l'Académie royale des sciences*, Paris, 1705.

[FRI 11] FRIEDEWALD M., RAABE O., "Ubiquitous computing: an overview of technology impacts", *Telematics and Informatics*, vol. 28, pp. 55–65, 2011.

[FUR 71] FURTH H.G., "Linguistic deficiency and thinking: research with deaf subjects 1964-1969", *Psychological Bulletin*, vol. 76, no. 1, pp. 58–72, 1971.

[GEL 86] GELLERMAN S.W., "Why "good" managers make bad ethical choices", *Harvard Business Review*, vol. 86, no. 4, pp. 85–90, 1986.

[GRU 05] GRUNDSTEIN M., "MGKME: a model for global knowledge management within the enterprise", *ICICKM 2005: 2nd International Conference on Intellectual Capital, Knowledge Management and Organizational Learning*, Bangkok, Thailand, 2005.

[GRU 12] GRUNDSTEIN M., "Three postulates that change knowledge management paradigm", in HOU H. (ed.), *New Research on Knowledge Management Models and Methods*, InTech, Rijeka, available at: http://www.intechopen.com/download/pdf/33406, 2012.

[GUO 11] GUO K., YUAN Y., ARCHER N. *et al.*, "Understanding Nonmalicious security violations in the workplace: a composite behavior model", *Journal of Management Information Systems*, vol. 28, no. 2, pp. 203–236, 2011.

[GYÖ 12] GYÖRY A., CLEVEN A., UEBERNICKEL F. *et al.*, *Exploring the Shadows: IT Governance Approaches to User-Driven Innovation*, ECIS, Barcelona, 2012.

[HAL 94] HALL R.I., AITCHISON P.W., KOCAY W.L., "Causal policy maps of managers: formal methods for elicitation and analysis", *System Dynamics Review*, vol. 10, no. 4, pp. 337–360, 1994.

[HEI 09] HEIDE L., *Punched-Card Systems and the Early Information Explosion*, Johns Hopkins University Press, Baltimore, 2009.

[ISO 13] ISO/IEC 27001, Management de la sécurité de l'information, ISO/IEC, 2013.

[JOH 13] JOHNSON S., "Bringing IT out of the shadows", *Network Security*, vol. 12, pp. 5–6, 2013.

[JON 11] JONES N.A., ROSS H., LYNAM T. *et al.*, "Mental models: an interdisciplinary synthesis of theory and methods", *Ecology and Society*, vol. 16, no. 1, 2011.

[KAP 82] KAPLAN S., KAPLAN R., "Attention and fascination: the search for cognitive clarity", in KAPLAN S., KALPLAN R. (eds), *Humanscape Environments for People*, Ulrich's, Ann Arbor, 1982.

[KAP 89] KAPLAN S., KAPLAN R., *Cognition and Environment: Functioning in an Uncertain World*, Ulrich's, Ann Arbor, 1989.

[KAS 15] KASPERSKY, Carbanak APT the great bank robbery, Technical report, Kaspersky Lab HQ, Russian Federation, 2015.

[KEA 97] KEARNEY A.R., KAPLAN S., "Toward a methodology for the measurement of the knowledge structures of ordinary people: the Conceptual Content Cognitive Map (3CM)", *Environment and Behavior*, vol. 29, no. 5, pp. 579–617, 1997.

[KEE 05] KEENEY M., KOWALSKI E., CAPPELLI D. *et al.*, *Insider Threat Study: Computer Systems Sabotage in Critical Infrastructure Sectors*, CERT, Software Engineering Institute, Carnegie Mellon University, 2005.

[KLA 89] KLAYMAN J., HA Y.W., "Hypothesis testing in rule discovery: strategy, structure, and content", *Journal of Experimental Psychology*, vol. 5, pp. 596–604, 1989.

[KLO 74] KLOCKARS C., "The professional fence", *Sociology*, vol. 10, no. 1, pp.174–175, 1974.

[KUH 70] KUHN T.S., "Reflections on my critics", *Criticism and the Growth of Knowledge*, Cambridge University Press, Cambridge, 1970.

[LAN 95] LANDAUER T., *The Trouble with Computers: Usefulness, Usability, and Productivity*, MIT Press, Cambridge, 1995.

[LAN 00a] LAND F., "The first business computer: a case study in user-driven innovation" *IEEE Annals of the History of Computing*, vol. 22, no. 3, pp. 16–26, 2000.

[LAN 00b] LANGAN-FOX J., CODE S., LANGGFIELD-SMITH K., "Team mental models: techniques, methods, and analytic approaches", *Human Factors*, vol. 42, no. 2, pp. 242–271, 2000.

[LAN 01] LANGAN-FOX J., WIRTH A., CODE S. *et al.*, "Analyzing shared and team mental models", *International Journal of Industrial Ergonomics*, vol. 28, pp. 99–112, 2001.

[LAU 77] LAURENCIN P., *Le Télégraphe terrestre, sous-marin, pneumatique; Histoire, principes, mécanismes, applications, règlements, tarifs, etc.*, J. ROTHSCHILD, Paris, 1877.

[LEV 98] LEVENSTEIN M., *Accounting for Growth, Information Systems and the Creation of the Large Corporation*, Stanford University Press, Stanford, 1998.

[LIE 08] LIEBOWITZ J., *Knowledge Retention: Strategies and Solutions*, CRC Press, Boca Raton, 2008.

[LOC 92] LOCH K., CARR H., WARKENTIN M., "Threats to information systems: today's reality, yesterday's understanding", *MIS Quarterly,* vol. 16, no. 2, pp. 173–186, 1992.

[LYN 02] LYNAM T., BOUSQUET F., LE PAGE C. *et al.*, "Adapting science to adaptive managers: spidergrams, belief models, and multi-agent systems modeling", *Conservation Ecology*, vol. 5, no. 2, pp. 24, 2002.

[MAT 11] MATHEVET R., ETIENNE M., LYNAM T. *et al.*, "Water management in the Camargue Biosphere Reserve: insights from comparative mental models analysis", *Ecology and Society*, vol. 16, no. 1, p. 43, 2011.

[MIT 03] MITNICK K., SIMON W., *The Art of Deception: Controlling the Human Element of Security*, John Wiley & Sons, Hoboken, 2003.

[MOR 02] MORGAN M.G., *Risk Communication: A Mental Models Approach*, Cambridge University Press, Cambridge, 2002.

[MUR 92] MURAKAMI Y., *Hankoten no keizaigaku*, Chuo Koron Sha, Tokyo, 1992.

[MUR 10] Murata K., "Lessons from the history of information system development and use in Japan", *Entreprises et Histoire*, no. 60, pp. 50–61, 2010.

[NOJ 05] Nojima H., "From everyday things to everyday memories: two kinds of interactions with objects in a house, ubiquitous computing systems", *Lecture Notes in Computer Science*, vol. 3598, pp. 10–19, 2005.

[NON 98] Nonaka I., Konno N., "The concept of "Ba": building a foundation for knowledge creation", *California Management Review*, vol. 40, no. 3, pp. 40–54, 1998.

[OZE 04] Ozesmi U., Ozesmi S.L., "Ecological models based on people's knowledge: a multi-step fuzzy cognitive mapping approach", *Ecological Modelling*, vol. 176, pp. 43–64, 2004.

[PAV 10] Pavlou P.A., El Sawy O.A., "The 'Third hand': IT-enabled competitive advantage in turbulence through improvisational capabilities", *Information Systems Research*, vol. 21, no. 3, pp. 443–471, 2010.

[PFL 02] Pfleeger C.P., Pfleeger S.L., *Security in Computing*, Prentice Hall, New Jersey, 2002.

[POL 67] Polanyi M., "Sense-giving and sense-reading", *Philosophy: Journal of the Royal Institute of Philosophy*, vol. 42, no. 162, pp. 301–323, 1967.

[POP 63] Popper K., *Conjectures and Refutations: The Growth of Scientific Knowledge*, Routledge, London, 1963.

[PWC 16] PwC, The Global State of Information Security® Survey 2016 – turnaround and transformation in cybersecurity, Report, available at: http://www.pwc.fr/the-global-state-of-information-security-survey-2016-turnaround-and-transformation-in-cybersecurity.html in 2018, 2016.

[QUI 05] Quinn N., "How to reconstruct schemas people share", *Finding Culture in Talk: A Collection of Methods*, pp. 33–81, Palgrave Miller, Basingstoke, 2005.

[REI 02] Reix R., *Système d'information et management des organisations*, Vuibert, Paris, 2002.

[RÉP 78] RÉPUBLIQUE FRANÇAISE, Loi no. 78-17 du 6 janvier 1978 relative à l'informatique, aux fichiers et aux libertés, JO du 6 janvier, p. 227, 1978.

[RIC 99] RICKHEIT G., SICHELSCHMIDT L., "Mental models: some answers, some questions, some suggestions", in RICKHEIT G., HABEL C. (eds), *Mental Models in Discourse Processing and Reasoning*, Elsevier, Amsterdam, 1999.

[RÖD 14] RÖDER N., WIESCHE M., SCHERMANN M., *A Situational Perspective on Workarounds in IT-Enabled Business Processes: A Multiple Case Study*, ECIS, Tel Aviv, 2014.

[ROO 78] ROOSEVELT C., *Instructions pour l'usage domestique du téléphone "Bell"*, Imprimeric Chaix, Paris, 1878.

[SCH 00] SCHNEIER B., "The process of security", *Information Security*, vol. 3, no. 4, p. 32, 2000.

[SHR 09] SHROPSHIRE J., "A canonical analysis of intentional information security breaches by insiders", *Information Management and Computer Security*, vol. 17, no. 4, pp. 221–234, 2009.

[SIL 14] SILIC M., BACK A.M., "Shadow IT – a view from behind the curtain", *Computers and Security*, vol. 45, pp. 274–283, 2014.

[SIP 10] SIPONEN M., VANCE A., "Neutralization: new insights into the problem of employee information systems security policy violations", *MIS Quarterly*, vol. 34, no. 3, pp. 487–502, 2010.

[STA 05] STANTON J.M., STAM K.R., MASTRANGELO P. *et al.*, "Analysis of end user security behaviors", *Computers & Security*, vol. 24, no. 2, pp. 124–133, 2005.

[STO 11] STONE-JOVICICH S.S., LYNAM T., LEITCH A. *et al.*, "Using consensus analysis to assess mental models about water use and management in the crocodile river catchment South Africa", *Ecology and Society*, vol. 16, no. 1, pp. 45, 2011.

[STR 98] STRAUB D., WELKE R., "Coping with systems risk: security planning models for management decision making", *MIS Quarterly*, vol. 22, no, 4, pp. 441–469, 1998.

[SUC 07] SUCHMAN L., *Human-Machine Reconfigurations: Plans and Situated Actions*, Cambridge University Press, Cambridge, 2007.

[SYK 57] SYKES G., MATZA D., "Techniques of neutralization: a theory of delinquency", *American Sociological Review*, vol. 22, no. 6, pp. 664–670, 1957.

[TCS 85] TCSEC, Trusted computer system evaluation criteria, Technical report, U.S.A National Computer Security Council, DOD standard 5200.28-STD, 1985.

[TSO 15] TSOHOU A., KARYDA M., KOKOLAKIS S., *et al.*, "Managing the introduction of information security awareness programs in organizations", *European Journal of Information Systems*, vol. 24, no. 1, pp. 38–58, 2015.

[TSU 93] TSUCHIYA S., "Improving knowledge creation ability through organizational learning", *ISMICK 1993: Proceedings of the International Symposium on the Management of Industrial and Corporate Knowledge*, Compiègne, France, pp. 87–95, 1993.

[TSU 99] TSUCHIYA S., "A search for new methodology to create a learning organization", *17th International Conference of the System Dynamics Society and 5th Australian and New Zealand Systems Conference*, available at: http://www.systemdynamics.org/conferences/1999/PAPERS/ PARA163.PDF, Wellington, New Zealand, 1999.

[WEI 79] WEICK K.E., *The Social Psychology of Organizing*, Addison-Wesley, Boston, USA, 1979.

[WEI 83] WEICK K.E., DAFT R.L., "The effectiveness of interpretation systems", in CAMERON K.S., WHETTEN D.A. (eds), *Organizational Effectiveness: A Comparison of Multiple Models*, Academic Press, New York, pp. 71–93, 1983.

[WEI 84] WEIZENBAUM J., *Computer Power and Human Reason*, Penguin, Harmondsworth, 1984.

[WHE 67] WHEELER J.A., Interview with Dr. John A. Wheeler By Charles Weiner and Gloria Lubkin, Princeton University, April 5, 1967.

[WIL 03] WILSON M., HASH J., "Building an information technology security awareness and training program", *NIST Special Publication*, vol. 800, no. 50, pp. 1–39, 2003.

[WIL 13] WILLISON R., WARKENTIN M., "Beyond deterrence: an expanded view of employee computer abuse", *MIS Quarterly*, vol. 37, no. 1, pp. 1–20, 2013.

[YAM 10] YAMAKAWA Y., NAITO E., "From physical brain to social brain", in PERUSICH K. (ed.), *Cognitive Maps*, InTech, Rijeka, 2010.

[ZIM 73] ZIMRING F., HAWKINS G., *Deterrence: The Legal Threat in Crime Control*, University of Chicago Press, Chicago, 1973.

Index

Advances in Information Systems Set

coordinated by Camille Rosenthal-Sabroux

Other titles from

in

Information Systems, Web and Pervasive Computing

2018

IAFRATE Fernando
Artificial Intelligence and Big Data: The Birth of a New Intelligence
(Advances in Information Systems Set – Volume 8)

MANDRAN Nadine
Traceable Human Experiment Design Research: Theoretical Model and
Practical Guide
(Advances in Information Systems Set – Volume 9)

2017

BOUHAÏ Nasreddine, SALEH Imad
Internet of Things: Evolutions and Innovations
(Digital Tools and Uses Set – Volume 4)

DUONG Véronique
Baidu SEO: Challenges and Intricacies of Marketing in China

LESAS Anne-Marie, MIRANDA Serge
The Art and Science of NFC Programming
(Intellectual Technologies Set – Volume 3)

LIEM André
Prospective Ergonomics
(Human-Machine Interaction Set – Volume 4)

MARSAULT Xavier
Eco-generative Design for Early Stages of Architecture
(Architecture and Computer Science Set – Volume 1)

REYES-GARCIA Everardo
The Image-Interface: Graphical Supports for Visual Information
(Digital Tools and Uses Set – Volume 3)

REYES-GARCIA Everardo, BOUHAÏ Nasreddine
Designing Interactive Hypermedia Systems
(Digital Tools and Uses Set – Volume 2)

SAÏD Karim, BAHRI KORBI Fadia
Asymmetric Alliances and Information Systems:Issues and Prospects
(Advances in Information Systems Set – Volume 7)

SZONIECKY Samuel, BOUHAÏ Nasreddine
Collective Intelligence and Digital Archives: Towards Knowledge Ecosystems
(Digital Tools and Uses Set – Volume 1)

2016

BEN CHOUIKHA Mona
Organizational Design for Knowledge Management

BERTOLO David
Interactions on Digital Tablets in the Context of 3D Geometry Learning
(Human-Machine Interaction Set – Volume 2)

BOUVARD Patricia, SUZANNE Hervé
Collective Intelligence Development in Business

EL FALLAH SEGHROUCHNI Amal, ISHIKAWA Fuyuki, HÉRAULT Laurent, TOKUDA Hideyuki
Enablers for Smart Cities

FABRE Renaud, in collaboration with MESSERSCHMIDT-MARIET Quentin, HOLVOET Margot
New Challenges for Knowledge

GAUDIELLO Ilaria, ZIBETTI Elisabetta
Learning Robotics, with Robotics, by Robotics
(Human-Machine Interaction Set – Volume 3)

HENROTIN Joseph
The Art of War in the Network Age
(Intellectual Technologies Set – Volume 1)

KITAJIMA Munéo
Memory and Action Selection in Human–Machine Interaction
(Human–Machine Interaction Set – Volume 1)

LAGRAÑA Fernando
E-mail and Behavioral Changes: Uses and Misuses of Electronic Communications

LEIGNEL Jean-Louis, UNGARO Thierry, STAAR Adrien
Digital Transformation
(Advances in Information Systems Set – Volume 6)

NOYER Jean-Max
Transformation of Collective Intelligences
(Intellectual Technologies Set – Volume 2)

VENTRE Daniel
Information Warfare – 2nd edition

VITALIS André
The Uncertain Digital Revolution

2015

ARDUIN Pierre-Emmanuel, GRUNDSTEIN Michel, ROSENTHAL-SABROUX Camille
Information and Knowledge System
(Advances in Information Systems Set – Volume 2)

PLANTIN Jean-Christophe
Participatory Mapping

VENTRE Daniel
Chinese Cybersecurity and Defense

2013

BERNIK Igor
Cybercrime and Cyberwarfare

CAPET Philippe, DELAVALLADE Thomas
Information Evaluation

LEBRATY Jean-Fabrice, LOBRE-LEBRATY Katia
Crowdsourcing: One Step Beyond

SALLABERRY Christian
Geographical Information Retrieval in Textual Corpora

2012

BUCHER Bénédicte, LE BER Florence
Innovative Software Development in GIS

GAUSSIER Eric, YVON François
Textual Information Access

STOCKINGER Peter
Audiovisual Archives: Digital Text and Discourse Analysis

VENTRE Daniel
Cyber Conflict

2011

BANOS Arnaud, THÉVENIN Thomas
Geographical Information and Urban Transport Systems

DAUPHINÉ André
Fractal Geography

LEMBERGER Pirmin, MOREL Mederic
Managing Complexity of Information Systems

STOCKINGER Peter
Introduction to Audiovisual Archives

STOCKINGER Peter
Digital Audiovisual Archives

VENTRE Daniel
Cyberwar and Information Warfare

2010

BONNET Pierre
Enterprise Data Governance

BRUNET Roger
Sustainable Geography

CARREGA Pierre
Geographical Information and Climatology

CAUVIN Colette, ESCOBAR Francisco, SERRADJ Aziz
Thematic Cartography – 3-volume series
Thematic Cartography and Transformations – Volume 1
Cartography and the Impact of the Quantitative Revolution – Volume 2
New Approaches in Thematic Cartography – Volume 3

LANGLOIS Patrice
Simulation of Complex Systems in GIS

MATHIS Philippe
Graphs and Networks – 2nd edition

THERIAULT Marius, DES ROSIERS François
Modeling Urban Dynamics

2009

BONNET Pierre, DETAVERNIER Jean-Michel, VAUQUIER Dominique
Sustainable IT Architecture: the Progressive Way of Overhauling Information Systems with SOA

PAPY Fabrice
Information Science

RIVARD François, ABOU HARB Georges, MERET Philippe
The Transverse Information System

ROCHE Stéphane, CARON Claude
Organizational Facets of GIS

2008

BRUGNOT Gérard
Spatial Management of Risks

FINKE Gerd
Operations Research and Networks

GUERMOND Yves
Modeling Process in Geography

KANEVSKI Michael
Advanced Mapping of Environmental Data

MANOUVRIER Bernard, LAURENT Ménard
Application Integration: EAI, B2B, BPM and SOA

PAPY Fabrice
Digital Libraries

2007

DOBESCH Hartwig, DUMOLARD Pierre, DYRAS Izabela
Spatial Interpolation for Climate Data

SANDERS Lena
Models in Spatial Analysis

Printed and bound by CPI Group (UK) Ltd, Croydon, CR0 4YY